Academic Language!

Academic Literacy!

A GUIDE FOR K–12 EDUCATORS

Eli R. Johnson

Foreword by Arthur L. Costa

CORWIN
A SAGE Company

For information:

Corwin
A SAGE Company
2455 Teller Road
Thousand Oaks, California 91320
(800) 233-9936
Fax: (800) 417-2466
www.corwinpress.com

SAGE Ltd.
1 Oliver's Yard
55 City Road
London EC1Y 1SP
United Kingdom

SAGE India Pvt. Ltd.
B 1/I 1 Mohan Cooperative
    Industrial Area
Mathura Road, New Delhi 110 044
India

SAGE Asia-Pacific Pte. Ltd.
33 Pekin Street #02-01
Far East Square
Singapore 048763

Printed in the United States of America.

Library of Congress Cataloging-in-Publication Data

Johnson, Eli R.
Academic language! academic literacy! : a guide for K-12 educators / Eli R. Johnson.
        p. cm.
Includes bibliographical references and index.
ISBN 978-1-4129-7132-4 (cloth)
ISBN 978-1-4129-7133-1 (pbk.)
    1. Academic language—Study and teaching. 2. Teachers—Language. 3. Communication in education. I. Title.

P120.A24J65 2009
370.14—dc22   2009012057

This book is printed on acid-free paper.

09   10   11   12   13   10   9   8   7   6   5   4   3   2   1

Acquisitions Editor:	Dan Alpert
Associate Editor:	Megan Bedell
Production Editor:	Veronica Stapleton
Copy Editor:	Adam Dunham
Typesetter:	C&M Digitals (P) Ltd.
Proofreader:	Susan Schon
Cover Designer:	Michael Dubowe

Contents

Academic Language! Academic Literacy! Strategy Matrix

Foreword

From the moment of birth (and even before), children are learning. Developing most rapidly from birth to three years of age, a child's brain absorbs massive amounts of information and stimuli. Deep inside a baby's developing brain, tiny neuro-circuits search for pathways to connect cells. Every taste, every touch, every interaction helps or hinders this process. Whenever a child is exposed to positive experiences, such as music, laughter, hugging, smiling, playing, and listening to loving voices, these connections form at an astonishing rate. Eventually, these neuro-circuits will help them speak, solve problems, and learn. But for that to happen, the circuits need to make good connections, and such connections depend on the quality of a child's earliest experiences. The more adults speak, sing, and read to the child, the faster the child's brain develops and the more a child learns. Positive interactions with humans and the environment result in the development of sound circuitry.

From birth, children begin to imitate sounds, then words, phrases, and thought patterns of the significant adults in their lives. As a result of these interactions, they develop the foundations of thought that endure throughout their lifetimes. Embedded in the vocabulary, inflections, and syntax of the language of adults are the cognitive processes and cultural values that are learned by children. Exposure to rich, fluent, varied, and complex language and thought enables children to handle complex thinking processes as they mature.

For some children, home life, however, is not that rich and supportive. In the past three decades there has been a significant transformation of the American family and the culture of youth. Growing up in an era of immediate gratification and bombardment with visual and oral stimuli, many a child's environment is characterized by increases in the amount of time passively spent watching television, playing videogames, listening to four-second sound bytes, surfing the Internet, and communicating through abbreviated text messaging.

With circumstances such as both parents working or traveling, single parenting, minors as parents, and "latch-key kids," the amount of face-to-face interaction in the modern family is vastly curtailed. Couple this with the burgeoning number of children whose primary language is other than English, with malnutrition, poor prenatal care, and the limited way their parents talk to them, and by the time many low-income preschoolers start school, they often have underdeveloped verbal skills.

Harried family life often lacks meaningful verbal interactions. What talk there is sometimes is bereft of complexity or deep meaning, and it often takes the form of interactions such as: "How was school?" "O.K." "What did you learn?" "Nothing." It frequently consists of terse commands: "Go to bed." "Do your homework." "Stop teasing your sister." "Eat your dinner." Furthermore, talk has become "cheap" with schlock jocks, rap, and "gutterances" from heavy metal sound blasts.

Indeed, recent neuroscientific research indicates that growing up in linguistically impoverished environments affects brain functioning. The neural systems of children from poor environments develop differently from those of more affluent children, which affects their language development and "executive functions," or the ability to plan, remember details, and pay attention in school.

Language and thinking are closely entwined. Like either side of a coin, they are inseparable. When you hear fuzzy, vague language, it is a reflection of fuzzy, vague thinking. Efficacious people strive to communicate accurately in both written and oral form, taking care to use precise language, defining terms, using correct names and universal labels and analogies. They strive to avoid overgeneralizations, deletions, and distortions. Instead, they support their statements with explanations, comparisons, quantification, and evidence.

Students grow up using vague and imprecise language to describe objects or events with words like *weird, nice,* or *O.K.* They identify specific objects with nondescriptive words such as *stuff, junk,* and *things.* They punctuate sentences with meaningless interjections like *ya know, er,* and *uh.* They use vague nouns and pronouns: "*They* told me to do it." "*Everybody* has one." "*Teachers* don't understand me." They use nonspecific verbs: "Let's *do* it." And they use unqualified comparatives: "This soda is *better;* I like it *more.*"

Preschool teachers may try to build children's vocabularies through word games, the taking of field trips, and parent workshops but find it difficult to close the gap between a child's expected and actual literary performance. Why these efforts often fail might be because the children have missed out on hearing millions of words in their first years of life. When children enter school lacking the complexity of language and thought needed to master academic demands, they are often linguistically deprived, cognitively disadvantaged, and, therefore, learning impaired.

Tony Wagner lists seven "survival skills" that students need to succeed in the information age, our 21st-century world, and he suggests that it's a school's job to make sure students have these skills before graduating.

1. Problem-solving and critical thinking

2. Collaboration across networks and leading by influence

3. Agility and adaptability

4. Initiative and entrepreneurship

5. Effective written and oral communication

6. Accessing and analyzing information

7. Curiosity and imagination

Each of these challenges has tremendous linguistic implications. Language refinement plays a critical role in enhancing a person's cognitive maps and their ability to think critically, which is the knowledge base for efficacious action. Enriching the complexity and specificity of language simultaneously produces effective thinking.

Success in school and future careers, therefore, is dependent upon skillful language usage. For example, effective problem solvers and critical thinkers must know how to ask questions.

"What evidence do you have . . . ?"

"How do you know that's true?"

"How reliable is this data source?"

"From whose viewpoint are we seeing, reading, or hearing?"

"From what angle, what perspective, are we viewing this situation?"

To be agile and adaptable, one must be empathic and listen with such understanding as to take another's point of view; one must be able to change one's mind with the addition of conflicting data and to admit one's errors.

To be collaborative, one must be able to accurately express, justify, and test the feasibility of his or her ideas and solutions on others. Through verbal interaction, groups and the individual continue to grow. Learning the art of compromise is a lifelong process that involves listening, consensus seeking, giving up an idea of one's own to work with someone else's, empathy, compassion, group leadership, knowing how to support group efforts, altruism—all are linguistic skills indicative of cooperative human beings.

Today's youth will succeed or fail depending largely on their dialogical skills whether within their career, organization, community, marriage, and family—their life. All forms of language—expressive language used in writing and speaking, and receptive listening and observational skills—are essential parts of being educated.

To meet these challenges, all educators and the community alike must attend to students' verbal, linguistic, and cognitive needs. Are these difficulties reversible, and are these 21st-century attributes achievable? Eli Johnson believes they are, given intentioned interventions to overcome these difficulties. This valuable book, therefore, provides teachers, staff developers, administrators, and teacher educators with a wealth of research-based practical knowledge, applications, instructional strategies, and assessments intended to help teachers become more aware of the language they employ in classroom interactions and to enhance their students' acquisition of academic language so as to maximize successful learning in school and in life.

Arthur L. Costa, EdD
Professor Emeritus
California State University, Sacramento

Acknowledgments

First and foremost, this book is dedicated to my wife, Shaunna, and to each of our wonderful learners at home: Natalie, Mikaila, Bryce, Erica, and Benjamin.

A special thanks goes to Art Costa, a great friend, whose encouragement and mentoring has been terrific. Also, Dan Alpert, Leigh Peake, and everyone at Corwin have been great. Doug Fisher deserves credit for initially planting the idea for this book. A big thanks goes to Alice Furry, Kathlan Latimer, Peter Finch, and Michelle Timmerman, who shared their educational experience and support. Appreciation also goes to all of my students, fellow teachers and administrators who have inspired and worked with me over the years.

In addition, I want to acknowledge all of the great researchers who have been such a great influence: Robert Marzano, Mary Schleppegrell, David Pearson, Margarita Calderon, Michael Kamil, Robin Scarcella, Nancy Kerr, Ed Kame'enui, Diane August, David Francis, Isabel Beck, Jeff Zweirs, Elfrieda Heibert, Russell Gersten, Betty Hart, Alison Bailey, Todd Risley, Kate Kinsella, Kevin Feldman, Louisa Moats, Catherine Snow, Lily Wong-Fillmore, and many others. To everyone, thank you!

Corwin wishes to acknowledge the following peer reviewers for their editorial insight and guidance.

Carol Gallegos, Literacy Coach
Hanford Elementary School District, Hanford, CA

Karen E. Janney, Principal
Montgomery High School, San Diego, CA

Kay Kuenzl-Stenerson, Literacy Coach
Merrill Middle School, Oshkosh, WI

Susan Schmidt, Principal
Chugiak Elementary School, Palmer, AK

Roselyne O. Thomas, Literacy Coach
Chapin Middle School, Chapin, SC

Teresa Tulipana, Principal
Hawthorn Elementary School, Kansas City, MO

About the Author

Eli R. Johnson is a consultant for the California Department of Education, supporting early literacy, English language professional development, and math and science projects. He works with urban districts throughout the state of California, strengthening teacher collaboration and school leadership. His previous experiences as a classroom teacher, site administrator, and instructional leader make him a valuable contributor to sustainable school reform. He earned a teaching degree from Brigham Young University and a master's degree in education from the University of Washington.

As a nationally recognized speaker and consultant, Eli works with teachers and leaders regarding the achievement gap, adolescent literacy, school leadership, and other issues affecting student achievement.

He is married to his wonderful wife, Shaunna, and they are the parents of five children: two in high school (Natalie and Mikaila), one in middle school (Bryce), one in elementary school (Erica,), and one in preschool (Benjamin). You can reach Eli at eli@achievement4all.com.

Academic Language and Academic Literacy

1

Literacy is at the heart of sustainable development . . . Acquiring literacy is an empowering process, enabling millions to enjoy access to knowledge and information which broadens horizons, increases opportunities, and creates alternatives for building a better life.

—Kofi Annan, 2001 Nobel Peace Prize Winner

Words are tools of learning. When words are organized effectively into language, they can become the most powerful tools in the world. Words can open up whole worlds of increased awareness and greater understanding. Words organize our actions and define us as humans. When used effectively, words contain the ability to inspire individuals and to lead nations. Words can have a tremendous impact on how people operate and learn. We also know that words act as the basic building blocks of language and learning at school. The words one chooses can create the leverage for a life of understanding and learning. Schools have their own special words and languages that coincide with the context and culture of learning. The words used in school should reveal the purposes and the pathways to success at school and beyond. So, what are the words in our schools that can have the longest lasting and greatest impact on student learning? The words that impact school the most are those that reveal *academic language.*

ACADEMIC LANGUAGE

Academic language is the formalized language of school. Academic language builds a foundation that helps our students define terms, form concepts, and construct knowledge. As key elements of academic language are emphasized and understood by all students, our schools will provide a more defined direction for learning. Dictionary.com defines the term *academic* as "Of or pertaining to college, academy, school, or other educational institution especially one of higher learning." *Language* is defined as "a body of words and the systems for their use common to a people who are of the same community or nation, the same geographical area, or the same cultural tradition." When used effectively in schools, academic language provides everyone a much clearer focus, so we, as teachers, communicate better, our students learn better, and our schools achieve better results. As we work together to improve academic language, each one of us can collectively impact student learning and make a significant difference in academic achievement. Creating this type of improvement within our schools takes a complete understanding of both the components and principles that make up academic language and academic literacy.

Academic language is becoming a more and more important issue in education because of the demands it places on our students to perform cognitively complex actions. For example, academic language includes words like *analyze, analyzing,* and *analysis; interpret, interpreting,* and *interpretation; compare, comparing,* and *comparison;* and *identify, identifying,* and *identification.* These words require that students understand complex concepts, take action, and engage in learning patterns that stretch their thinking and learning abilities to greater heights. Gersten and colleagues (2007) define *academic language* as "the language of the classroom, of academic disciplines (science, history, literary analysis), of texts and literature, and of extended, reasoned discourse. It is more abstract and de-contextualized than conversational English" (p. 23). Students need significant academic language support to scaffold their learning for greater understanding. Hu (2008) shares the following story, which tells one student's tale of academic language and academic success at one struggling school.

Hakim's Story

Relief turned to satisfaction that Newton was not just another failing school with low test scores. This time, nearly 80% of its fourth graders had passed math, 69% language arts, and 77% science, all double-digit increases from the previous year, and one of the biggest overall gains in the Newark school system. Buried beneath the numbers were hard-won victories by students like Hakim McKenzie, 10, who repeated third grade this year. The third-grade scores also rose, with 56% passing math and 67% language arts (there is no third-grade science test). Hakim failed the math test last year because he did not understand the questions, stumped by words like "estimate" and "reduce." This year, he not only passed math but also scored high enough to earn an "advanced proficient" designation. "It's the first thing I've been good at," said Hakim, a shy boy with a toothy grin who has earned the nickname Little Teacher among his classmates because he helps them with math homework. "My friends say, 'How did you get that good in math?' I say that I use books and my teacher, Mr. Kilgore, helps me. I feel like I've achieved something really good." (p. A1)

Knowing key academic language words like *estimate, reduce, analyze,* and *conceptualize* support student's abilities to be successful in school. If our schools are going to meet the literacy demands of an increasingly challenging global environment, then academic language must be understood and mastered by all learners (Wong-Fillmore, 2007). Furthermore, academic language is important to academic literacy and the reading comprehension of students as they engage in textbooks, narrative stories, and informational texts. Academic language provides us an essential framework for developing our student's formal literacy skills for both school and career. Understanding the types of academic language and developing content-area literacy are necessary skills for constructing the learning resources that everyone needs to succeed in today's schools.

LANGUAGE GAP

As we very well know, no issue in education seems to grab people's attention today more than the *academic achievement gap.* The achievement gap describes many of the differences between the achievement results by students in low socioeconomic circumstances versus their peers. Large numbers of students in poverty are often two grade levels or more behind their peers, and a lack of academic language affects their achievement at school. Closing the achievement gap has become both a moral imperative for our students and an economic imperative for our country. Hirsch (2003) notes, "It is now well accepted that the chief cause of the achievement gap between socioeconomic groups is a language gap" (p. 22). Most definitely, the language of learning at school is an academic language that is both precise and purposeful. Using academic language effectively means that we help learners recognize the function of language, the structure of language, and the demands of language in our classrooms. Pollock (2007) notes that the academic language of school needs to be very clear and we should use "precise terminology to describe what students will learn" (p. 3). The more accurate and precise the language used by teachers, the more students will understand the purposes of school. If our students are unable to comprehend the words and grasp the academic concepts that serve as a bridge for learning, then our students will face an ever-increasing, uphill battle in school.

LITERACY GAP

Developing powerful literacy for all of our students is at the heart of closing the achievement gap. Many students personally express that they sorely lack the language and literacy structures to succeed in school (Moats, 2000). The academic literacy gap exists because so many students of poverty struggle with basic literacy skills, and these students lack the literacy strategies to succeed. Pinkus (2008) notes the importance of literacy and learning:

> Literacy is the gateway skill that students must have mastered if they are to be successful in any course; low literacy levels translate into poor grades, grade repetition, and eventual disengagement from school, all of which tend to precede a student's decision to drop out. (p. 4)

The achievement gap, which may be measured by a myriad of different assessments, reveals a large gap in literacy that separates student success from student frustration. Without the academic literacy skills to read, write, and communicate with confidence, our children will struggle to compete academically now and financially in the future. Students definitely feel the pressure created by the increasing gaps in their literacy and achievement. Every one of our students must fully develop a framework of academic literacy so that they can assume a place of learning and leadership within our communities and within the global economy.

ACHIEVEMENT GAP

Gaps in language lead to larger gaps in literacy and learning, and gaps in literacy and learning lead to gaps in achievement. When students fail to fix gaps in their language and learning, these gaps often widen and become chasms where students eventually drop out and are academically lost. Most important, our students need to develop academic language and literacy skills so that they can participate effectively in content-area classrooms, in our democratic society, and in the global economy. The lack of academic language has created a dire situation for so many of our students who come from poverty. Elmore (see Crow, 2008) notes that the achievement gap finds at its core a language gap: "In Boston, we've got about 40% of the population who . . . don't have the academic vocabulary needed to do the work" (p. 46). Directly stated, the language gap leads to a literacy gap, while the literacy gap leads to a gap in academic achievement. As the conditions grow more desperate, students need a systematic and strategic plan to directly increase their academic language and literacy, or many of them will be lost. Needless to say, American education will only realize its tremendous potential when we put language and literacy in their proper place within every classroom. If our students never get a grip on the academic language and literacy of the classroom, they will lose their grip on their educational opportunities and may never seem to hold onto life's opportunities.

TWO CATEGORIES OF ACADEMIC LANGUAGE

Most important, understanding the language of learning at school is the beginning of building an academic foundation and framework for achievement. Overall, academic language includes two primary categories, which are critical for succeeding in school: *specific content language* and *general academic language*. The first category covers the particular terminology of a specific subject matter. Specific content language includes the specialized terms that are unique to math, science, language arts, and social studies, or those used within other school subjects. The second category of language covers the general academic language that cuts across all of the content areas at school. General academic language is commonly referred to as *academic language*. Academic language engages students in the key actions and processes of learning. Academic language develops necessary cognitive connections within the minds of our students and simultaneously develops their internal structures of knowledge (Marzano, 2004). Knowledge structures provide the schemata or background information needed to develop further conceptual knowledge. Academic language can help each student build deeper comprehension and connect concepts across the curriculum at school. Specific content language develops our students' depth of learning, while general academic language develops their breadth of learning.

(Specific) Content Language (Bricks)

First of all, specific content language is the type of academic language at school that sets math, science, language arts, social studies, and other subjects apart from each other. Specific content language provides our students with the challenge of learning the key terms and concepts of a particular subject matter. The prospect of learning specific content language increases in difficulty as our students advance through each grade level and the subject matter becomes more narrow in its focus. The narrowing of focus also leads to a greater depth of understanding. It takes a focused effort for students to learn the academic terminology that can be used as the key resources for developing concepts within a specific content area.

In addition, specific content language provides the essential building blocks from which conceptual knowledge can be built. The more a student understands the specific content language of a particular subject matter, then the faster and more efficient they can learn additional knowledge (Willingham, 2006). Providing explicit instruction in language at school is often seen as a domain only for the language arts class; yet, each subject area has its own unique academic language demands that it places on students. These specific language demands set each content area apart from other disciplines and make each discipline unique. Following are examples of content-area language.

Types of Specific Content Language

- **Social Studies** (i.e., *democracy, civilization, communism, geography,* and *legislature*)
- **Mathematics** (i.e., *fraction, equation, division, angle, addition,* and *factor*)
- **Science** (i.e., *photosynthesis, friction, compound, plate tectonics,* and *force*)
- **Language Arts** (i.e., *alliteration, plot, genre, author's voice, theme,* and *irony*)

Let's look at comments from several authors as they outline a few of the specific content-language challenges found in various core subjects.

Ogle, Klemp, and McBride (2007) outline several language challenges: "Social studies texts also contain a great deal of academic vocabulary—content-specific terminology with meanings specific to history or government. Social studies texts are filled with abstract '-isms' about economics, religion, government, and culture" (p. 14).

Schleppegrell (2007) notes that "Learning mathematics and the language of mathematics is a challenge for all students, but is especially challenging for students who have no opportunities to use academic language outside of school" (p. 141).

Bailey, Butler, Laframenta, and Ong (2004) emphasize the importance of academic language for science educators: "During science lessons, teachers exposed students to academic language within a range of instructional contexts" (p. 24).

As we have noted, specific content language serves as a basic building blocks for learning. Specific content language strengthens the depth of our student's conceptual understanding within a discipline. Learning specific content language will help our students throughout their school career and will open up more options and opportunities in a chosen field of work (Hambrick & Oswald, 2005). In college, students select a chosen field of study, and this choice often leads to a job in a chosen profession like engineering, journalism, psychology, or physics. As our students progress in their academic careers from high school to college, the academic language becomes more specific and precise. Knowing the specific content language of various disciplines can lead to greater success for our students in school and beyond.

(General) Academic Language (Mortar)

General academic language provides a foundation for educational success. The more academic language our students know and use, then the stronger their foundations become. The words included in general academic language act like mortar or cement. These words hold and bind specific content-area language and concepts together within the minds of students. General academic language helps our students cement the building blocks of specific content language into conceptual knowledge that in turn produces both educational and real-world results. Academic language includes the many words that connect concepts, outline transitions, and demonstrate relationships. General academic language—or what we will refer to going forward as *academic language*—cohesively connects the abstract concepts of school. It differs significantly from the social language of home and the playground. Chamot and O'Malley (1994) describe academic language as "the language that is used by teachers and students for the purpose of acquiring new knowledge and skills . . . imparting new information, describing abstract ideas, and developing students' conceptual understanding" (p. 40). Developing academic language requires students to engage in abstract actions and organize complex concepts, and it is the nature of uniting these ideas that makes academic language cognitively challenging for all learners.

Academic language is powerful because of its ability to integrate and tie together many important concepts in the various content areas. For example, terms like *consider, evaluate, synthesize, revise, compare,* and *determine* are academic words that can be applied to every content area. Knowing how to use this academic language in each class subject helps all students see how learning is integrated throughout school. As we have noted, academic language acts as both the mortar for cementing the building blocks of specific content language together and as a scaffold for concept development. Look over the three types of academic language that serve as cohesive devices that develop academic coherence for our student's learning.

Types of Academic Language

- **Actions** (i.e., *recognize, monitor, analyze, connect, achieve,* and *require*) as verbs, holds sentence together
- **Transitions/Relationships** (i.e., *in addition, first, in fact, furthermore, nonetheless,* and *finally*) holds ¶ tog.
- **Concepts** (i.e., *abstraction, function, repertoire, evidence,* and *features*) → holds topic together paper/project

Let's look, for example, at the concepts associated with the terms *analyze, analyzing,* or *analysis* as we consider the importance of academic language. Our students are asked to analyze a variety of information at school, yet many of them may have little explicit understanding of this term or how it is used. The word can be particularly difficult for our English language learners, special education students, or the socioeconomically disadvantaged. As learners are repeatedly taught this key academic word in several classes, they can begin to recognize the importance of this word to their success at school. In a mathematics class, the concept of *analyzing* is developed in ways that look at problem solving. In a science class, the concept of *analysis* is a key part of investigation. Language arts classes encourage *analyzing* the characterization traits of human nature in the context of the human condition in literature. Social studies classes *analyze* the causes and effects of war on the economic, social, and political systems of a country. When our students learn that the term *analyze* simply refers to a method for breaking their learning down into parts, then they can see how the term is used in various subject areas.

As our students learn how to mentally classify or categorize items into parts and see patterns of relationships through the process of analysis, they are better prepared to accomplish the learning tasks assigned in school. Making sure that every student understands academic language terms, like *analyzing,* provides each student a much richer experience and a greater opportunity for academic success. Knowing the academic language that is expected in school can produce powerful results because the skill of analyzing carries over to so many academic challenges and career contexts. Academic language connects the learning processes within academic disciplines and helps learners access the language of professions. As we will discuss further in Chapter 2, academic language cohesively cements specific content language into meaningful sentences, paragraphs, and essays by providing the actions, relationships, transitions, and concepts that unite ideas.

AN ACADEMIC CHALLENGE

How can we grasp the importance of helping our students fully recognize the value of explicitly learning academic language? Let's take some time and look at the challenges that face so many of our students who have difficulty with academic language. The following example is a mathematics question taken from a California Standards Test (National Testing Services, 2007) for sixth graders. Please take a minute and read the question carefully as many times as needed and then write down your answer. After writing down your answer, record next to it your level of confidence that you have correctly answered the question.

> *Solamente queda un pedazo en que se puede construer, y el cine ocupara todo eso completamente. En ese frase, la palabra pedazo significa*

A. mucho de algo

B. un grupo complete

C. una seccion de tierra

D. la resulta de un chance

Answer _____   Confidence _____%

Most educators, when presented with this question, unless they are fluent in Spanish, find that although they love learning, their persistence and motivation drops sharply as they face the academic demands made by this question.

Let's attempt the question one more time, now with some of the words translated into English. Take a minute to read the question thoroughly and determine which answer is correct. Again, write in your answer and record what level of confidence you have in your answer.

Only remains *un pedazo en* question *se puede construer, y el* theater occupied all *eso* space. *En ese* sentence, the word *pedazo* means

A. great amount

B. complete group

C. section of land

D. result of chance

Answer _____   Confidence_____%

Think briefly how you might feel about school if each question on a test or daily classroom activities offered more of these same challenges. We know that motivation and self-confidence greatly affect rates of learning. What happens to your motivation and confidence as you face these questions? Typically, educators respond that their confidence and motivation are diminished dramatically, and the realization that academic language is so closely tied to our ability to convey knowledge becomes evident. Remember that for English language learners, academic language is the third register that they are asked to develop (the first is their native language; the second is English). If you would like the correct answer to the preceding question, please turn to the end of this chapter.

ACADEMIC LANGUAGE DEMANDS

As educators, we sometimes take for granted the demands that language can make on learning. Most of us enjoyed the process of school and succeeded with its language demands. Becoming more aware of the language demands that the rigors of successful schooling can place on each learner helps us recognize the increasing needs of our students to learn academic language consistently and comprehensively. When a reading passage contains a high degree of language complexity and a high degree of academic language density, then the language is said to have a high degree of academic demand (Bailey & Butler, 2003). In fact, this paragraph may be more challenging to read than the headlines in a daily newspaper, as it contains elements of academic language that are cognitively abstract, structurally complex, and conceptually dense. In upcoming chapters, we will discuss strategies for developing student comprehension in textbook passages that contain academic language with a high degree of academic complexity and density.

Furthermore, academic language contains the words that sentences are predicated upon, as well as the words that coherently connect concepts and integrate related ideas. As previously mentioned, academic language can be separated into three types of functions or word types: *action words, transition/relationship words,* and *concept words.* Action words reveal internal processes, and they function in ways that expect the reader to think about learning (Swartz, Costa, Beyer, Regan, & Kallick, 2007). The transition words included in academic language are those that signal text-based transitions and identify conceptual relationships. The concept words included in academic language are those that connect complex ideas together. As we progress throughout the book, the term *academic language* will refer to the words and language patterns that help to reveal the cognitive actions, text-based transitions, and complex concepts of powerful learning.

ACADEMIC CASUALTIES

The current reality is that students who only know the casual language of the neighborhood and streets most often become casualties of an educational system that neglects to ensure academic language is learned and academic literacy is developed. Academic casualties lack the physical wounds of real war, yet they are essentially handicapped when it comes to advancing in professions where formal language is an operational necessity. We find significant numbers of these students eventually dropping out of school and becoming casualties of the achievement gap. The national average for dropout rates throughout the country is currently nearing 30%. In inner city high schools and high-poverty rural areas, the dropout rates are often above 50%. Why do we have such tremendously high dropout rates, particularly among poor minorities? When asked, these students have shared that a lack of literacy skills tops the list of factors that influenced their academically fatal decisions. Consider the following facts regarding school dropouts:

- Every school year, 1.2 million of our youth drop out of high school (Alliance for Education, n.d.). The most commonly cited reason is the lack of literacy skills to negotiate the demands of school (Kamil, 2003; Snow & Biancarosa, 2003).
- Students who enter the ninth grade with academic language and literacy skills that are in the lowest quartile are 20 times more likely to drop out of school than the highest performing students (Carnevale, 2001).
- Over 40% of African-American students and 45% of Hispanic students fail to graduate from high school with their peers (Orfield, Losen, Wald, & Swanson, 2004).
- More than 75% of school dropouts mentioned that difficulties in their ability to read in core classes significantly contributed to their decision to drop out (Lyon, 2001).
- Far greater numbers of American workers need the basics of reading, writing, speaking, and listening to support the in-depth knowledge, intellectual creativity, and mental flexibility that is required in our current economic landscape (Kirsch et al., 2002).

The facts from the research reveal how far we have to go in providing a language foundation for all students, particularly for those students that are English language learners, economically disadvantaged, or racial minorities. At a time when intellectual capital is at a premium, our schools are seeing increasing dropout rates. Bill Cosby (Cosby & Poussaint, 2007) states very directly, "Let's face it—the high dropout rate for black students is related in part to poorly developed language skills, and this shortcoming keeps getting bigger and bigger over the years" (p. 61). Recognizing the intertwining connections between academic language, socioeconomic disadvantage, school dropouts, and the achievement gap has become crucial for all educators. As our students learn academic language, they will increase their abilities to succeed in school and increase the likelihood that they will remain in school rather than become another statistical casualty.

IMPROVING ACADEMIC LANGUAGE AND LITERACY

Whether you are a teacher leader, site leader, or district leader, you can more fully develop your understanding of academic language. Stronge (2007) highlights a major connection between a classroom teachers' language skills and student learning, "One key finding has emerged: students taught by teachers with greater verbal ability learn more than those taught by teachers with lower verbal ability" (p. 15). The more a teacher uses and models academic language with students, the better the students will achieve academic results. Improving the abilities of all educators to effectively model and instruct academic language will provide a foundation for social justice and support a framework for academic literacy for each student.

A major goal of this book is to help you, as an educational leader in your classroom and school, provide all students with the academic language to negotiate the challenges of literacy and learning. So many of our students enter school with gaps in their language skills, and they lack the ability to identify the terms and understand the concepts that will help them learn effectively and efficiently at school. These students need explicit instruction in academic language and engaging classroom experiences in academic literacy. This book will help you accomplish three things as an educational teacher and leader. After completing this book you will be able to

1. Develop a greater understanding of academic language and be able to model explicit instruction in academic language to support your students every day.

2. Learn current and confirmed methods that show how to explicitly support student learning in academic language and academic literacy for all students.

3. Engage students in specific classroom strategies that will improve academic literacy through reading, listening, speaking, and writing.

ACADEMIC LANGUAGE TOOLS AND RESOURCES

In addition, this book contains one very exciting resource—an inclusive list of academic words that every student should learn at each grade level to develop their language of learning. Appendix I provides teacher leaders *Academic Language Grade-Level Lists* for each elementary grade, K–6, for each middle school grade, 7–8, and for each high school grade, 9–12. These thirteen lists provide key words and lay a foundational model for supporting academic language within schools. They have been designed to serve as a starting point for developing a systematic program for instruction in academic language, concepts, and patterns. Additionally, Appendix II highlights several *specific content language resources* for each grade level, K–12. These specific content language lists can provide you, as a teacher leader or school leader, a common reference point for developing your own specific content-area language lists that will best fit the academic needs of your particular school, classroom, and individual students.

SUMMARY

As we have discussed, when educators engage their learners in the foundational elements of academic language, a framework for academic literacy can fully develop for all students. The specific content-area language serves as the building blocks for learning, while the academic language acts as the mortar which cements these chunks of knowledge together. As students like Hakim and others increase their ability to construct meaning using the bricks of specific content language and the mortar of academic language, they will find their ability to succeed in school significantly improves. Research links academic language, academic literacy, the achievement gap, and dropout and graduation rates together. Unfortunately for socioeconomically disadvantaged children, the dynamics cycle in a downward spiral that often leads to significant gaps in achievement and overwhelming dropout rates. Knowing the casual language of the streets without knowing the academic language of school can cause students to become academic casualties. Our schools can be transformed as we scaffold instruction and provide strategies that reveal the academic language of cognitive actions, text transitions, and complex concepts. As instructional leaders, we can generate greater academic results when we create a culture of learning around academic language and align and integrate academic literacy for every student.

PERSONAL REFLECTIONS

1. How often do I provide instruction in both specific content language and general academic language?

2. How do I use my knowledge of language and learning to reduce the academic achievement gap?

3. What strategies do I provide my students to improve their literacy in grade-level content?

P.S. As you read through the upcoming chapters, you will discover a simple-to-follow framework for developing academic language in the classroom as well as powerful strategies for developing academic literacy throughout your school and district. As you proceed, you may decide that you want to jump right into the classroom literacy strategies, so feel free to go directly to Chapter 4. On the other hand, you may want to gain a more complete understanding of academic language and literacy and move sequentially through Chapters 2 and 3. Or, you may decide you are tempted to turn to the academic grade-level lists and sneak a peek in the appendix. Whichever way you decide to proceed, enjoy the journey!

The answer to An Academic Challenge is C, una seccion de tierra [a section of land].

Academic Language and Learning 2

Language is the blood of the soul into which thoughts run and out of which they grow.

—Oliver Wendell Holmes

Mai Xi's Story

Before she was born, Mai Xi's mother and father made the treacherous trek with their family across the countryside of Laos. They were escaping the communist government newly instated by the North Vietnamese Army. In the mountains of Laos, Mai Xi's father had fought in the war against the Vietnamese. He and many of his fellow Hmong backed America's secret war in Southeast Asia. In return for their support, the U.S. government had promised the Hmong that they would receive schools for their children. When the United States suddenly pulled out of Southeast Asia, the Hmong people lost their ally and were considered war enemies of the Vietnamese. Living in daily peril, Mai Xi's parents traveled at night across the Laos countryside carrying her brother, then just a baby. When they reached the Mekong River, which separated their homeland from the safety of Thailand, they hastily constructed a log raft and became part of those fortunate to make it safely across.

Life in Thailand meant living in a refugee camp. Mai Xi was born in one of these constantly overcrowded camps. As she grew up, she saw many of her relatives leave the camp for America, yet her father insisted on staying near Laos with the hope that they would one day be allowed to return to their homeland. As years past, Mai Xi grew up in the weary existence of the camp, and the hopes of returning to the mountains of Laos seemed to fade. The only life Mai Xi had ever known was within the meager refugee camps. Mai Xi had never attended school—in the camp, an education was considered a luxury, and one had to pay for the privilege. Instead of attending school, she stayed home and helped care for her younger brother. In 2004, when Mai Xi was a teenager, news came that the Thai government made an agreement with the U.S. government that the last remaining refugee camp would be closed. Mai Xi and her family would leave Southeast Asia and fly to America.

Their family was relocated to California, where uncles, aunts, and other relatives lived. Upon landing in Fresno, fourteen-year-old Mai Xi walked off the jet plane and entered an entirely new world. She, and others who had to leave when the camp was finally closed, now had the opportunity to go to school. An education was free for the taking, yet it came at

(Continued)

(Continued)

a price. High school was taught in an entirely different language and conducted in an entirely different culture. Mai Xi attended school faithfully every day, as she slowly began learning the casual conversation that would allow her to venture into the community. Her first year of high school was full of many new experiences. Learning to speak and write even simple words and sentences became a tangible measure of achievement. By the middle of her second year in high school, Mai Xi was officially designated a sophomore, and her parents were very pleased with her progress at school. She had accomplished so much, yet she still had so far to go.

LEARNING ACADEMIC LANGUAGE

Once students like Mai Xi learn the casual language needed to communicate in the community, they then need to learn the academic language that will help them function effectively in school. Academic language requires accuracy and precision. As we'll discover throughout the book, talking the talk at school means that both teachers and learners recognize and use academic language effectively. Whether the subject is math or science, language arts or social studies, all students can learn the academic language that takes learning to the next level. As the ability to construct accurate and precise language increases, the ability to understand more complex concepts also increases (Costa & Kallick, 2000). As your students master the academic language of school for themselves, they will be better prepared for advancement to the next grade level, for graduation to the next school, and eventually for a successful career.

ACADEMIC LANGUAGE AND ACADEMIC FOUNDATIONS

More than ever, academic language is foundational for success in school. It is the language of learning itself. Throughout the organization of school, academic language is woven into the literacy expectations of a high-quality education. As educators, most of us have been immersed in the language of school since we started kindergarten. Thus, we often take for granted the way we use language to define our thoughts and convey our educational objectives. As educators, academic language was easy for most of us to learn; and those of us who needed extra effort were likely able to persevere until we grew fluent.

Although most children enter school with at least the basic ability to speak the casual language of the community, they lack the academic language that will help them succeed in school. Consider some of the differences between casual conversational language and formal academic language (see Table 2.1).

Table 2.1 Conversational Versus Formal Academic Language

Casual Conversational Language	Formal Academic Language
Relies on facial expressions and gestures to relate content	Relies on language structure to relate content
Uses voice inflection and tone to convey meaning	Uses precision of words to convey meaning
Shares information that is familiar and related to interests	Shares new information related to a formal topic
Addresses more concrete and tangible information	Addresses more abstract and general information
Focuses on a current context here and now	Focus is decontextualized from here and now

Helping our students become proficient in the more challenging academic language of school will help them throughout their lives.

ACADEMIC LANGUAGE: A LANGUAGE OF STANDARDS

Academic language provides the common threads that make up the content standards. As each state developed the standards in the four core-content areas of language arts, mathematics, science, and social studies, they consistently drew upon key academic language terms. Hinkel (2005) notes the connection between the standards and academic language, "Standards reflect what students should know and be able to do within the various subjects, and, therefore, make assumptions about uses of academic language" (p. 705). Nearly every state content standard uses academic language like *define, explain, analyze, recognize,* and *identify* to outline curricular objectives (Bailey & Butler, 2003). Most definitely, our students need to understand and master the academic language required by state standards. We know that standards help coordinate curriculum, inform instruction, and improve assessment. Pull a copy of the standards off the shelf and examine the types of words that direct the learning for each standard. Consider the following examples of state content standards provided in California (National Testing Services, 2006) to help students prepare for the annual state assessments:

Second-Grade Mathematics

SS2.0   Students *estimate, calculate,* and *solve* problems involving addition and subtraction of two- and three-digit numbers.

Tenth-Grade World History

WH10.4   Students *analyze* patterns of global change in the era of New Imperialism in at least two of the following regions or countries: Africa, Southeast Asia, China, India, Latin America, and the Philippines.

Fifth-Grade Science

5IE6.   Scientific progress is made by *asking* meaningful questions and *conducting* careful investigations. As a basis for *understanding* this concept and *addressing* the content in the other three strands, students *develop* their own questions and *perform* investigations. Students will: *classify, develop, plan, identify, select, record, draw,* and *write.*

Eighth-Grade Language Arts

8RW1.0   Word analysis, fluency, and systematic vocabulary development: Students *use* their knowledge of word origins and word relationships, as well as historical and literary context clues, to *determine* the meaning of specialized vocabulary and to *understand* the precise meaning of grade-level appropriate words. (adapted from National Testing Services, 2006)

When our students understand the various dimensions of academic language and learn to engage in academic literacy practices, they will improve their abilities to meet the performance levels expected by state standards.

ACADEMIC LANGUAGE: A LANGUAGE OF CURRICULUM

Academic language is also woven throughout the language of content curriculum. Christie (1985) reveals that the demands made by academic language are part of the "hidden curriculum" of our schools. Because these challenges are encapsulated in the language of curriculum, it can be difficult for our students to see the many ways that academic terminology and concepts increase expectations for learning. Cummins (2000) acknowledges that

> Language is infused in all areas of the curriculum and is the medium through which instruction and assessment are carried out. While academic language proficiency is implicated to a greater extent in some areas of the curriculum than in others (e.g., Language Arts compared to Mathematics), it represents an important dimension even in relatively "non-verbal" areas. (p. 163)

Public school curricula make requirements of students that have only increased in complexity and difficulty. These increasing language demands have stretched both educators and students alike during an era where state and federal standards expect everyone to achieve. In science courses, curriculum guidelines use academic language terms like *discuss, describe, guide, method, suggest, specify,* and *provide* to accomplish state standards. The Science Framework for the California Department of Education (2004) states, "Effective science programs develop student's command of the academic language of science used in the content standards" (p. 10). Effective curricular programs in all content areas encourage students to acquire a command of academic language.

ACADEMIC LANGUAGE: A LANGUAGE OF INSTRUCTION

For educators across the country, academic language is the language of quality classroom instruction. Instruction is the crucial process that fuels learning. It requires active involvement and high engagement by our students. Explicit instruction in academic language will strengthen our student's capacity to more easily connect concepts and create comprehension. Bell (2003) adds these insights for improving instruction: "Teach and consistently incorporate into your questions words that have been shown to trip up at-risk students on standardized tests. Some of these words include *analyze, infer, trace, explain,* and *contrast.*" As the instruction in our schools improves through language and literacy in all curricular content areas, then student learning will also improve. Classroom research has observed the following conditions regarding instruction and academic language (adapted from Snow & Kim, 2007):

- Educators rarely provide academic vocabulary instruction.
- Instruction, when it is provided, covers discipline-specific language rather than general academic language.
- Academic language is crucial for understanding textbooks and academic texts.
- Textbooks can be difficult and unengaging without instructional support in academic language.
- Classroom discussions that support academic language are rare.
- Students need repetition and recurrent exposures to academic language.

Additionally, instructional objectives that incorporate academic language should be clear, precise, and challenging for students. Quality instruction needs to be carefully crafted and consciously delivered in ways that makes learning academic language an explicit goal for our students.

Classroom instruction focusing on academic language connects the various strands of state standards, content-area curriculum, and school assessments together for greater student success. In the end, daily explicit instruction that engages learners in academic language will help all of our students create the capacity to achieve literacy success in school and beyond.

ACADEMIC LANGUAGE: A LANGUAGE OF ASSESSMENT

In an era of proficiency for all students, academic language is the language of assessment. Assessment has become an increasingly weightier matter for all of us. It has become the norm, and the results are heavily scrutinized. Statewide assessments, exit exams, year-end assessments, and senior course exams, all contain questions grounded in academic language. These tests strive to accurately assess challenging and complex concepts, so the questions asked must contain clear and precise terminology. According to Ballard and Tighe (2007), "Academic language plays an equally important role in the area of assessment because children must know how to express what they know to take content-specific tests" (p. 1). Test makers purposely design questions around academic language terms to create consistency with the state standards.

Stevens, Butler, and Castellon-Wellington (2000) state in their research on assessment, that "Implicit in the work reported here is the notion that academic language underlies the content matter constructs being tapped by the large-scale assessments or at least that academic language is the conduit of the concepts being tested" (p. 4).

ACADEMIC LANGUAGE: THE LANGUAGE OF TEXTBOOKS

Textbook publishers, in their efforts to meet the high expectations of standardized education, have increased the language demands of these formal volumes. The textbooks produced in the past five years contain a wealth of knowledge, yet increased expectations in academic language means the textbooks are more challenging. Most students develop the basic skills to decode and comprehend texts in the early elementary grades, yet many struggle with comprehending and connecting the concepts in middle and high school textbooks (Kamil, 2003). Sirota (2007) notes that "Many students in high school are well versed in speaking English, but they are not necessarily well versed in the academic language of textbooks so they may have a hard time understanding the textbooks" (p. 1). With challenging texts, our students are expected to understand academic language terms and develop multiple connections in their conceptual understanding. Consider the following passage from Rinehart and Winston's (2006) 10th-grade *Modern Biology:*

> Even though van Leeuwenhoek had *published* reports about his many discoveries, the scientific community *failed* to *recognize* the microscope's significance for many years. In 1773, an amateur optician named Chester Moor Hall found a way to *solve* the persistent problem of chromatic aberration in compound lenses, and in 1774, the technique was *applied* to microscopes. By the 1820s, new types of microscopes were available, and the 1800s and 1900s *brought* frequent improvements. In 1931,

the first electron microscope was *invented,* and in 1981, the scanning tunneling microscope began to *reveal* objects atom by atom. Today's work in microbiology, protozoology, bacteriology, and other fields *depends* on advanced microscopes, descendants of those simple lenses through which van Leeuwenhoek first saw his "animalcules." (p. 85; emphasis added)

The preceding paragraph contains many academic language words that required abstract actions of scientists. When students are asked to engage with these abstract concepts, like *invent, reveal, solve, depend,* and *recognize* as well as the concrete actions *publish* and *apply,* they can quickly become aware of the significant challenges executing academic language can present. As learners progress in a particular discipline, the specificity and complexity of the content knowledge increases. Textbooks often are organized in a particular fashion, and they are designed to connect various concepts together. Paragraphs in textbooks organize patterns of information together to help students learn content ideas in detail. Snow (2002) notes that

readers who are unaware of text structure do not approach text with any particular plan of action. Consequently, they tend to retrieve information from the text in a seemingly random way. Students aware of text structure, on the other hand, tend to 'chunk' or organize the text they read. (p. 40)

The language of textbooks gets more advanced as children progress through school, and the complexity of sentence and paragraph structure also increases. Students need to be explicitly engaged in the academic language of textbooks so they can successfully face the rigors of high standards.

ALIGNING ACADEMIC LANGUAGE AND LEARNING

We all know the importance of curriculum, instruction, and assessment for improving student learning. A primary challenge of any classroom is to connect quality curriculum with quality instruction, and then to connect quality instruction with quality assessment (Drake, 2007). In so many ways, academic language provides the fundamental threads that help to align state standards, school curricula, classroom instruction, and formal assessments. As our students become aware of the fact that academic language is a common element in curricular texts, instructional standards, and assessment exams, they will see more relationships between what they are learning and how their learning is connected. Systematically infusing academic language and academic literacy into each classroom allows curriculum, instruction, and assessment to become aligned in meaningful ways, and it allows our students to see greater coherence in their education. Language, particularly academic language, strengthens our own ability to extend, expand, and elaborate our learning, and it can do the same for our students. Some students may be several grade levels behind, yet quality instruction in academic language can improve their abilities to succeed in school. When our students receive explicit instructional support in academic language, then curriculum becomes more coherent, instruction becomes more powerful, and assessment results are more easily achieved. Now, let's consider another story that looks at some of the issues our students face.

Tyrese's Story

Tyrese disliked most of his experiences at school. He went to school, it seemed, only because his mom demanded nothing less. His mom would remind Tyrese that she almost graduated from high school until she became pregnant with him and dropped out her junior year. She seemed to bring up the matter whenever she would reflect on her limited job opportunities. She wanted better for Tyrese, and he thought he did too. Yet, his first year of high school was extremely difficult. The homework seemed harder, and the textbooks were confusing. If it hadn't been for PE and Beginning Art and a couple of nice teachers who gave a lot of second chances, his grades would have been terrible. Tyrese thought about dropping out like his cousin, yet he wanted to make his mom proud. It seemed that every day he got further and further away from knowing what was going on in his classes.

During Tyrese's sophomore year, his school started something called *small learning communities,* and his teachers would talk about "getting training" every couple of months. Listen as he summarizes his thoughts on this time in school: "In my second year of high school the teachers began meetin' together every week, so we got to sleep in and go to school later in the day. All the teachers started talkin' in class about the types of words we used at school. We had to start answerin' them in complete sentences, and we had to do somethin' the teachers called 'structured academic talk.' It was way annoyin.' The teachers gave us words to start our sentences so that when we discussed somethin' we would speak right. We had to write a lot more and we had to do a lot of stuff with our school books to make sure we knew what we were learnin'. At first it seemed dumb and fake to be tryin' to say all of this fancy stuff, but then it started to kinda make sense. My grades started to go up, and goin' to class seemed more fun. We did a lot more talkin' in class, and the teachers would really listen to us. They would correct us if we messed up and make sure we said things right. I began to like it way better. Ms. Williams even called my mom and told her I was doin' good. She was super happy."

In the two stories about Mai Xi and Tyrese, we can see they have extremely different background experiences, yet they do have several things in common. They both struggle with the language demands of textbooks that are increasingly more difficult. They both face significant gaps in their reading and writing skills. They are both expected to take a standardized test at the end of the year and pass a state exit exam before they will be able to graduate from high school. Both Mai Xi and Tyrese will continue to benefit from understanding how the three different types of academic language impact their learning.

ACADEMIC LANGUAGE: A LANGUAGE OF COGNITIVE ACTIONS

Academic language, when properly implemented in the classroom, transforms students from passive recipients into active participants. Academic language is demanding, because it expects students to take action. Academic language requires our students to *define, analyze, compare, synthesize,* and *create.* Academic language expects students to first cognitively process actions internally and then, through external actions, to *reveal, demonstrate, showcase, state, document,* and *illustrate* their knowledge. Every day we ask our students to engage in cognitive actions in our classrooms so they can progress and learn. Many of these actions can be readily observed, while others are internal actions happening within each individual learner (See Table 2.2).

Table 2.2   Examples of Cognitive Actions

Internal Actions	External Actions	Social Actions
Think	Perform	Listen
Infer	Write	Present
Comprehend	Describe	Demonstrate
Consider	Diagram	Show

Academic Language words require active effort on the part of the learner. The actions called for by academic language are cognitive processes that occur within the learner. Learners are expected to apply themselves to the academic actions, and these actions lead to the production of academic knowledge. Academic language is powerful and at the same time challenging because it expects so much of the person using the language. When our students turn internal actions into external results, the results can be observed by others in the classroom.

ACADEMIC LANGUAGE: A LANGUAGE OF TEXT TRANSITIONS

Additionally, academic language is a language of text transitions. It includes transition words and phrases such as *to begin with, most important, first, for example, whereas, although, given that, despite,* and *such as,* which demonstrate important text connections.

Students in kindergarten use basic transition words like *and, but,* and *yet* to combine sentences and make comparisons. As students enter middle school, they face a number of transitions. This is a great time to make sure these students understand additional transition language like *therefore, whenever,* and *initially.* Middle school students should also learn to use these transition words to help organize their writing. Consider the words in Table 2.3, which help students transition as they read text and recognize relevant relationships among ideas.

Wong-Fillmore (2007) encourages teachers to work on words that express logical relationships such as, "if, because, therefore, however, unless, same, alike, different from, opposite of, whether, since, unless, almost, probably, exactly, not quite, always, never, and so on. These are critical to understanding academic texts because these words are used to link ideas" (p. 6). Academic language provides the glue that connects ideas and identifies transitions in classroom text.

Table 2.3   Examples of Text Transitions

Priority Transitions	Additive Transitions	Causal Transitions
First and foremost	Furthermore	Resulting in
Most important	In addition	Influenced by
Ultimately	Moreover	Because
Significantly	Additionally	Consequently

ACADEMIC LANGUAGE: A LANGUAGE OF COMPLEX CONCEPTS

Academic language is also a language of complex concepts (see Table 2.4). Academic language includes complex concepts like *variable, reflection, issue, hypothesis, strategy,* and *component,* which operate at a generalized and abstract level. These words express ideas that are quite different from the common nouns that are used to name persons, places, and things. As Cummins (2000) points out, academic language is decontextualized, while casual conversation tends to be about tangible things in the here and now. Because these abstract academic processes are intangible and nonconcrete, they can be much more challenging to grasp and comprehend for students. Costa and Kallick (2000) address the challenges:

> Learning progresses through stages of increasing complexity (the number of ideas and factors we can think about) and increasing abstraction (progressing from a concrete object to a pictorial representation of the object, to a symbol that stands for the object, to a spoken word that stands for the symbol). (p. 4)

As students advance in their academic careers, the number of complex concepts increases at each grade level.

Academic language is used in school to describe complex thinking processes, often called higher-order thinking skills. These include cognitive processes that are used to comprehend, solve problems, and express ideas (Swartz, Costa, Beyer, Regan, & Kallick, 2007). Social studies covers abstract, content-specific concepts like *freedom, economy, capitalism,* and *democracy.* Mathematics contains content-specific concepts like *square-root, function, mean,* and *exponent.* Science contains content-specific concepts like *variable, atom, catalyst,* and *kinetic energy,* while concepts like *symbolism, analogy, interpretation,* and *theme* are abstract concepts in language arts. Making sense of these complex concepts can prove difficult for many students. Academic language can be challenging because of a variety of factors: the abstract nature of these words, the transitional nature of these words, and the conceptual nature of the words. As our students understand the academic language that signals complex concept patterns, then learning will become much easier for our students.

Table 2.4 Examples of Complex Concepts

Abstract Concepts	System Concepts	Tangible Concepts
Autonomy	Strategy	Technology
Purpose	Associations	Evidence
Freedom	Culture	Resources
Principle	Process	Committee

ACADEMIC LANGUAGE FUNCTIONS

At its roots, all language serves a function or a primary purpose for being expressed to others. Many of us may remember the Saturday morning songs for learning about different language functions. One of these School House Rock songs is still memorable from Saturday mornings many years ago, *"Conjunction junction what's your function . . . hooking up words, phrases, and clauses"* (see Newall & Eisner, 2002). Understanding the function of a word can help to explain how words operate within sentences and supports meaning. Understanding the functions of language helps learners develop greater awareness of the purposes for which language is used. The language functions in casual registers are most often focused on tangible conversations about here-and-now events as well as items of personal interest. On the other hand, the language functions of academic registers demand abstract action and the connection of complex concepts (Halliday, 1994). Actions, transitions, and concepts function as the cohesive elements that connect ideas together. *Actions* bind the various words and ideas in sentences together; *transitions* and *concepts* bind the various words and ideas in paragraphs and larger text passages. It is precisely the cohesive nature of academic language that makes it an almost hidden, yet crucial, element of high-quality student learning. Our students benefit when they can identify the various functions of words and determine how they cement learning and create meaning. Language functions outline the academic purposes, direct the academic intentions, and represent the academic tasks of school. The cohesive quality of academic language helps to join, connect, link, relate, weave, and chain concepts together.

ACADEMIC LANGUAGE AND INSTRUCTIONAL DESIGN

Academic instruction benefits from purposeful design that uses academic language to build the content knowledge students need. Effective instructional design includes the academic purposes and tasks that communicate to students the direction their learning should take. To achieve rigor, quality lesson design emphasizes academic assignments or tasks that use academic language to fulfill abstract and tangible actions. Schleppegrell and Colombi (2002) note that

> The register features required for academic assignments differ in significant ways from the registers of ordinary spoken interaction, making it necessary for even those students whose English is already well developed for everyday tasks to expand their linguistic repertoires and learn to be more precise in their linguistic formulations to meet the demands of school based tasks. (p. 120)

When we design instruction that stretches students to higher levels of rigor and cognitive demand, then they will be able to meet the challenges of the classroom, college, and a career. Design matrices outlining the purposes, intentions, and tasks of academic language functions are provided in the next section to help guide the construction of lesson plans to improve academic language instruction. Tables 2.5 through 2.8 provide lesson design structures and examples for incorporating the academic purposes, academic intent, and academic tasks at various levels of difficulty. They're intended to help in organizing instruction and assessing learning. Notice the academic language terms used to outline the purposes, intent, and tasks that students are expected to demonstrate and master.

The academic design matrices will you help prepare and develop classroom instruction that supports literacy and learning. When students recognize how academic language functions reveal a pattern of academic purposes, academic intent, and academic tasks, then they will be able to function more effectively in school. The academic tasks of school use academic language that requires students to engage in *abstract actions, text transitions,* and *complex concepts* to achieve the purposes of education and function effectively within school.

Table 2.5 Academic Instructional Design Matrices

Basic Design Level: These academic actions are the basic steps that students take to begin learning.

Academic Purposes of Language Functions	Academic Intent (expects students to be able to)	Academic Tasks (identified by academic language)	Examples of Academic Classroom Activities
Seek Information	• Observe and explore • Acquire new information • Inquire or question	Select, label, identify, count, draw, indicate, list, match, name, recall, record, read, define, ask, repeat, trace, wonder, listen, inquire, note, attribute, consider	• Ask who, what, where, when, and how to gather new insights • List words that describe a bird • Take notes from the PowerPoint presentation on fractions
Infer	• Predict implications • Hypothesize • Make inferences	Deduce, guess, predict, derive, connect, relate, give examples, determine, recognize, represent, summarize, construct, logic, hypothesize, generalize, extrapolate	• Identify the reasoning process (inductive or deductive) to arrive at a conclusion • Generate a hypothesis to determine causes and outcomes
Inform Others	• Identify and provide a clear description • Report on an activity • Share with a partner	Tell, depict, state, conclude, describe, speak, recount, declare, summarize, give examples, share, draw, explain, convert, prepare, write, transform, relate, paraphrase	• Retell a story in your own words • Develop a brief report • Describe the main character to your neighbor • Summarize Chapter 2

Table 2.6 Intermediate Design Level

These academic actions are designed to help students engage and extend their learning.

Academic Purposes of Language Functions	Academic Intent (expects students to be able to)	Academic Tasks (identified by academic language)	Examples of Academic Classroom Activities
Analyze	• Break down the whole into parts • Identify complex relationships and patterns	Recognize, select, subdivide, separate, detect, reclassify, deduce, identify, determine, results, pinpoint, criteria, recalculate, reorder, rearrange, relate, investigate	• Take a water sample from the river and identify any indicators of pollutants • Identify the six parts of the conflict plot pattern in the story • Analyze all aspects of the functions and determine if they are congruent

(Continued)

Table 2.6 (Continued)

Academic Purposes of Language Functions	Academic Intent (expects students to be able to)	Academic Tasks (identified by academic language)	Examples of Academic Classroom Activities
Synthesize	• Combine items in new patterns to make a new whole • Integrate several new ideas together	Rearrange, design, compile, construct, develop, reveal, reorganize, compose, derive, combine, retell, formulate, modify, plan, propose, revise, transmit, interpret, devise, summarize, transform	• Share your ideas and plan for reducing air pollutants • Show how you would arrange these colors and shapes into a new pattern • Share with your group three ideas for improving learning in our classroom
Persuade	• Provide a particular point of view • Encourage others to agree	Convince, illustrate, review, debate, thesis, rhetoric, argue, convey, present, include, revise, showcase, reference, explain, relate, recommend, propose	• Write a letter to the editor about preserving the environment • Conduct a debate about who should be the next president and ask students to vote • Prepare a speech about the benefits of college

Table 2.7   Complex-Combinations Design Level

These academic actions are combinations of analysis, synthesis, and persuasion from the intermediate design level.

Academic Purposes of Language Functions	Academic Intent (expects students to be able to)	Academic Tasks (identified by academic language)	Examples of Academic Classroom Activities
Compare and Contrast	• Describe similarities • Identify differences in objects or ideas	Distinguish, compare, describe, point out, illustrate, attributes, commonalities, contrast, identify, recognize, separate, differentiate	• Use a Venn diagram to show how _____ and _____ are the same and different • Describe _____ vs. _____
Order and Sequence	• Determine ranking • Sequence events, objects, or ideas	Organize, develop, choose, complete, discover, determine, complete, rank, process, outline, order, rate, place, select, arrange	• Make a timeline of key battles in the Civil War • Provide the sequence of the story • Describe the stages of mitosis

Academic Purposes of Language Functions	Academic Intent (expects students to be able to)	Academic Tasks (identified by academic language)	Examples of Academic Classroom Activities
Classify and Categorize	• Group objects or ideas according to features (size, shape, color, etc.) • Recognize basic relationships between items	Generate, include, classify, discriminate, criteria, relate, group, identify, determine, differentiate, construct, represent, correlate, sort, patterns, recognize, characterize	• Identify each animal as a reptile, insect, or mammal • Describe five systems of the human body and their functions • Look at the list of 25 words and determine whether they originate from Greek, Anglo-Saxon, or Latin

Table 2.8 Advanced Design Level

These academic actions help students to engage at advanced levels of cognitive and metacognitive learning.

Academic Purposes of Language Functions	Academic Intent (expects students to be able to)	Academic Tasks (identified by academic language)	Examples of Academic Classroom Activities
Justify	• Determine the thinking of a decision • Give reasons for one's actions	Distinguish, document, reason, support, validate, decide, preclude, relevance, verify, evidence, conclude	• Outline for the principal your reasons for starting a student store • Show examples that support your results
Create Solutions	• Define the possibilities • Determine a solution • Represent a course of action • Generate the solution	Solve, make, hypothesize, deduce, act, construct, produce, succeed, predicate, become, accomplish, achieve, overcome, exemplify, generate	• Describe what you can do to improve your grades • Figure out a way to power a vehicle without using gasoline • Show three different ways you can solve the equation
Assess	• Determine the value of an object, idea, or decision • Evaluate the situation or results	Appraise, evaluate, distinguish, grade, judge, validate, test, measure, monitor, rank, determine value, check	• Read five essays, and write about your favorite one • Tell us who has been the best U.S. President and share why

THE ROLES OF ACADEMIC LANGUAGE

Academic language provides students a method for understanding the key components of the core content areas in school and for expressing their thinking within these subjects. Francis, Rivera, Lesaux, Kieffer, and Rivera (2006) note that "Academic language becomes increasingly important with increasing years of schooling, as students read to acquire concepts, ideas, and facts in content-areas such as math, science, and social studies" (p. 15). Consider the following list of statements that complete the sentence frame, and see if you can add any to the list.

Academic language is _____.

- used in *state standards*
- used in *content-area curriculum*
- used in *explicit instruction*
- used in *educational assessment*
- used in *classroom textbooks*
- made up of *abstract actions*
- made up of *text transitions*
- made up of *complex concepts*

- made up of *academic functions and tasks*
- found in *higher-order thinking*
- found in *content reading*
- found in *academic talk*
- found in *cohesive understanding*
- found in *structured writing*
- a language that *reveals relationships*
- a language that *supports future professions*

Quality instruction immerses students in engaging language, and it is important for our students to increase their awareness of the accumulative effects that developing academic language can have on their overall learning experiences and future success.

SUMMARY

Academic language is the powerful language of learning and making meaning. In many ways, academic language provides the common thread that is found in all core content areas and woven throughout core standards, curriculum, and assessment. On the one hand, casual language can help transitioning students, like Mai Xi, interact with peers in lunch lines, yet it falls far short of providing students the skills to negotiate the textbooks, assessments, and learning demands of school. On the other hand, our students can all succeed in school, as we make sure they understand the crucial role academic language plays in quality learning.

Academic language can be difficult to learn and fully grasp because it contains abstract actions, text transitions, and complex concepts that are each cognitively challenging. The cohesive quality of academic language makes it a vital link for supporting our students as they make sense of their learning. Creating instructional coherence helps students to function effectively in rigorous academic settings. Many inner city youth, like Tyrese, find that negotiating the language functions of the classroom can be far more difficult than negotiating the language challenges of street rapping on the neighborhood corner. As our students recognize the language functions, understand the instructional intent, and engage in the academic tasks required in rigorous learning, then they will be prepared to fully grasp content-area concepts. Formal education uses academic language to provide a foundation for high-quality standards, curriculum, instruction, and assessment in school. When we design instruction that builds a foundation of academic language and supports a framework of literacy for each student, then our students will be able to weather the academic tests of time.

Acquiring the language of quality classrooms ultimately requires that all of our students develop the academic language of learning. As our students become skilled in the core components of academic language, they will be able to weave the threads of curriculum, instruction, assessment, and state standards into a cohesive fabric of learning that will endure long into the future.

PERSONAL REFLECTIONS

1. How do I make sure my students are aware of the academic language of content-area textbooks, state standards, successful instruction, and common assessments?

2. How do I help my students recognize specific content-area language and all three types of academic language: abstract actions, text transitions, and complex concepts?

3. In what ways do I design lesson plans so that students fully develop their academic language, literacy, and learning?

Academic Literacy Challenges 3

Throughout America's history, education has been the vehicle for social and economic mobility, giving hope and opportunity to millions of people of all ages. We must break the cycle of children for whom poverty is their inheritance and illiteracy their destiny.

—Barack Obama

Many of our students possess strong literacy skills when they enter our classrooms. They are able to read at grade level and easily keep pace with instruction. At the same time, other students struggle to obtain the basic literacy skills needed to succeed in the core content areas of school. All of our students are routinely tested, even though many of them have difficulties with the basic reading, speaking, and writing skills. In our current world, effective literacy skills have increasingly become necessary tools for success. The issue is particularly pressing for many students from impoverished homes who struggle to comprehend core textbooks, engage in meaningful discussions, and write about classroom content. We know that students can succeed academically, and each deserves an equal opportunity to achieve. As our students develop their language and literacy abilities, they will be able to progress on the road to a successful future.

ACADEMIC LITERACY

Academic literacy is directly connected to our current economic reality and has become an essential requirement for success in the world. Literacy strengthens our ability to engage with others and expands the number of concepts we can consider and communicate. Moxley and Taylor (2006) provide us with the following definition of academic literacy: "Literacy is defined as listening, viewing, thinking, speaking, writing, and reading and expressing through multiple symbol systems at a developmentally appropriate level" (p. 12). Opportunities await students who acquire academic language and engage in consistent academic literacy practices across the content areas. The National Association of State Boards of Education (2005) report notes that "Literacy is the linchpin of standards-based reform . . . the explicit instruction of literacy skills in the context of content-area learning supports student achievement not only in reading and writing, but across the curriculum" (p. 5). Students need a daily diet of academic literacy activities to help them digest the content contained in textbooks at school and strengthen their ability to perform on tests. A highly celebrated five-year study revealed that a fully implemented literacy program of instruction across content areas is critical for students' sustained educational success (Earle et al., 2003). Instead of being an add-on program, this type of literacy instruction is infused into the content, activities, and practices that currently exist in school. Fullan (2007) states, "If you had to name one thing that every school should do well, you would have to consider teaching deep literacy as standing head and shoulders over all other priorities" (p. 7). Developing academic literacy through listening, speaking, reading, and writing increases our students' ability to learn and to scaffold a framework for a brighter future.

POVERTY AND ACADEMIC LITERACY

Poverty continues to impact learning outcomes for many of our students. Most definitely, poverty compromises students' ability to learn without difficulty. The odds are often stacked against children in impoverished homes before they ever arrive at school. Poverty rates in America are in fact growing, and they affect minorities in greater numbers. Crary (2008) notes that poverty rates are increasing: "The national rate was 11% for white children, 36% for blacks and American Indians, and 28% for Hispanics" (p. 2), with the highest rates in the inner-city areas." Over 80% of children who are experiencing long-term poverty, often passed from generation to generation, are African-American (Tough, 2008). The higher rates of poverty among minorities can bring socioeconomic and racial inequities into our schools. These inequities significantly affect language, literacy, and learning.

The quality of conversations and quantity of language used in many homes and classrooms creates a potential divide that places many students at a significant literacy disadvantage as they go through school. Consider the following story about classmates George and Julie (adapted from Fielding, Kerr, & Rosier, 2007), which contrasts the very different experiences many of our students face.

George and Julie's Story

George was unaware that he was entering school with fewer words than his classmates. Instead, he came to kindergarten with new shoes, a bright smile, and his parents' eager hopes for him, yet he only possessed the language skills of the average three year old. At the same time, Julie, with her own bright smile, a new outfit, and her parents' eager hopes, arrived with the literacy skills typical of a five year old. George and Julie loved kindergarten, and both sets of parents anticipated bright futures for them. Yet, unlike George, Julie had been read to frequently at home, and she spent a lot of her time with books before entering school. She thinks she just reads for fun—and she does—but in the process, she is quietly piling up more words, language, and concepts that will help her learn even more. She is reinforcing and strengthening her background knowledge and the skills that will increase her comprehension and fluency. On the other hand, George definitely needs to increase his language skills or else he will fall further behind. He will need targeted strategies and literacy support in every subject area if he stands a chance of reducing the gaps in his learning. George knows that he struggles to read and write, yet his lack of skills makes him reluctant to engage in reading and writing as he falls further behind. George continues to struggle as he enters middle school and the gap in language grows even larger.

For Julie, doors appear to be opening as her solid communication skills help her progress in school. These same doors seem to be closing for George. Looking at the numbers, it seems George reluctantly reads only rarely inside or outside of school. Julie, on the other hand, has read about one million words each year outside of school. As she enters high school, Julie looks to be on cruise control. George, as a sophomore, quite reluctantly, is reading at a seventh-grade level. Increasingly, George finds ways to disengage at school.

He becomes painfully aware that he is behind—not only in reading but also in every other subject. He cuts classes here and there and struggles to complete his homework. He failed one class first semester and is flunking three more in his second semester. The school counselor notifies him that time is quickly slipping away, and he definitely needs to step up his game. He decides to really hit the books, yet it seems like they will just hit back. He knows he lacks much of the language to comprehend textbooks, to master classroom content, or to pass school tests. In contrast, Julie passes all of her classes and has good grades for participation in extracurricular activities. After finding out she passed her college entrance exams, Julie has been accepted to several local universities and she is still deciding on a major for her future. Unfortunately, George realizes graduating with his peers is no longer going to happen for him. Instead, he considers how much a minimum wage job pays and how much his future hopes and dreams have dimmed.

George's experience has become a recurrent story for many of our students, for whom disadvantages and struggles increase over time. Breaking the cycle of poverty as President Obama has encouraged will require a strategic approach to bridging gaps in academic language and literacy. The daily actions of teachers can counteract the accumulated disadvantages in language development. Research shows that content-area teachers, who enjoy large vocabularies and use formal academic language in their instruction, produce greater academic achievement for their students (Stronge, 2007).

DEVELOPING LITERACY

Literacy begins by obtaining the basic ability of comprehending the written word. Once students have developed decoding skills and have learned to read, they then need to further develop the academic vocabulary and language that is essential in reading to learn. Even though most every student develops the basic ability to read or decode language, many of them lack the academic language and literacy skills to comprehend their reading assignments at grade level. The compounding effects of this frustrating situation accumulate as students enter middle school and move on to high school. Reading to learn has its own unique challenges in each of the content areas. Gee (2001) observes that "more children fail in school, in the long run, because they cannot cope with 'academic language' than because they cannot decode print" (p. 2). Once students have developed the ability to decode language and read at basic levels, then they need to be given opportunities to engage in literacy strategies and practices that will enhance, extend, and expand their learning. Students often do well learning to read, yet many of them struggle as they are required to read to learn. Reading to learn provides students with the skills to grasp challenging text and the complex concepts contained in written text. Reading to learn is supported by listening and speaking comprehension, and it helps lead to effective writing skills.

Reading to Learn

- *Academic Listening Comprehension* develops as students increase awareness of discussions and actively direct their attention to others' expressions.
- *Academic Speaking Comprehension* develops our student's ability to express themselves about various content areas in school.

- ***Academic Reading Comprehension*** develops as students understand the various meanings different words, phrases, and passages present.
- ***Academic Writing Comprehension*** develops our students' ability to record and share their thinking and conceptual understanding for others to consider.

Improving instruction will help our students engage in each of the literacy practices of learning: reading, writing, listening, and speaking. The four key areas of learning through literacy help develop our students' comprehension of content-area concepts. When these literacy skills are taught effectively and explicitly to our students in all content areas, then our students can bridge the literacy gap and succeed in school at each grade level. Increasing academic intensity, or the level at which literacy expectations and academic language is required of students, effectively narrows the achievement gap between ethnic groups and increases learning for all students (Coleman, 1990). Filling the cracks in our students' language foundations with the cement of academic language will decrease our students' difficulties and increase their opportunities.

LITERACY AND LANGUAGE REGISTERS

At an early age, little children begin to learn words and develop language patterns by observing and listening to their parents, other adults, and older siblings. As the sounds that make up words and various languages are nurtured, children also begin to develop a language register that matches the context of home and the culture of the community. The structure and scope of individuals' language patterns and their background knowledge within a specific context is called a *language register* (Bailey, 2007). The language registers of students can differ greatly in their form and content. Cummins (2000) notes the difference between social language registers that are acquired for everyday casual communication compared to academic language registers that require greater cognitive demands. Language registers are unique in their lexicons, functions, and structures (Halliday, 1994). Within the same language, individuals may develop more than one language register. The primary language registers that individuals develop are casual language registers. Schleppegrell (2004) describes the challenges of learning a new language register: "The learning of new registers, like learning a second language, requires appropriate input, opportunities for interaction and negotiation of meaning, and relevant focus on the form that language takes in different settings and as its is used for different tasks" (p. 13). All language registers take attention, effort, and practice to develop. But it is well worth the demands of time, energy, and patience as our students will benefit from learning multiple language registers. Language registers differ because they have a separate slang, jargon, or lingo that makes each one unique.

Within each language register are different subcategories that have unique contexts, terminology, structures, and patterns that set them apart. Because the specific language register subcategories differ, they actually require register development that almost seems like a separate language. For example, the text messaging that so many students use to communicate requires a separate language register. The acronyms, slang, symbols, and cryptic language used in texting create its own category of communication. Texting requires a language register be learned and developed to interpret and understand what is being communicated via cell phone or computer. Take for example the following message.

AYT ? WYD T+ YTG TNT LY

Note that this very casual language register of texting has little language structure and a very unique terminology that sets it apart from other language registers. When translated into a standard language register this message reads, "Are you there? I have a question. What are you doing? Think positive; you're the greatest. Until next time, I love you. End of message." Our students are very comfortable communicating in text with this unique type of casual language register, yet texting has limited benefits at school.

Types of Language Registers

To develop our students' understanding, language registers can be separated into three general categories: casual language registers, academic language registers, and professional language registers. Each language register takes effort to develop; and the language register that succeeds at a dinner party may be quite different from the language register that succeeds in a U.S. history classroom or a corporate boardroom. Just as learning several different languages can be a significant advantage for an individual, developing multiple language registers can also provide significant benefits.

As our students understand and develop their language registers, they will discover that the more language registers one knows, the easier they will develop others. Casual language registers developed at home can help individuals develop academic language registers at school, and academic language registers can help individuals develop the professional language registers of the workplace. The research shows that many careers are becoming more technically specific, and higher-paying jobs make more language demands of their employees (Barton, 2003). Developing formal terminology and academic language registers goes a long way toward developing professional language registers that can be critical for our students' professional futures. The slang of casual language, the jargon of academic language, and the lingo of professional language set each language register apart as uniquely different.

> **Three Categories of Language Registers**
>
> 1. Casual Language Registers: home, neighborhood, hobbies, and friends
>
> 2. Academic Language Registers: school, formal writing, and college
>
> 3. Professional Language Registers: jobs, politics, and work-related conversations

Casual Language Registers

Initially, casual language registers develop within the context of home. As individuals go into the community and develop their own special interests, they may recognize and start to develop other casual language registers based on a particular sport, culture, or activity. Sports like baseball, football, and cricket have a language all their own that use much of the language of other English language registers, yet these sports' words, phrases, and language structures differ significantly from other casual language registers (Trosborg, 1997).

For example, read the following sports page headline: *"THE CATCHER STOLE THIRD AND THEN CROSSED HOME ON A SACRIFICE FLY FOR THE WIN!"* This simple statement may be easy to understand for an individual who has a well-developed baseball language register, yet it may seem like complete nonsense to a goat herder from South Africa who knows nothing about baseball.

In addition, a casual language register is most often a language of speaking or listening, and it is used to communicate with family, with friends, and with others in casual settings. The casual language of the street may be rich and descriptive, and in the context of a weekend social event can be most appropriate. Casual language registers can help students negotiate lunch lines and make friends, yet it falls far short of providing these students the ability to negotiate the textbooks, assessments, and learning demands that require a high level of academic language. The African-American vernacular is an example of a casual language register that is embedded in a cultural context (Rickford, 1999; Baugh, 2000). This vernacular provides its own words, language functions, and language structures, and it is useful for communicating on the streets and between friends. Yet it poorly prepares students for the academic rigors in courses that will prepare them for work. In speaking of the differences between language registers, actor Bill Cosby (Cosby & Poussaint, 2007) acknowledges that "no translator at the UN can tell you what 'fo'shizzle, ma nizzle' means. Hanging on to such styles in school can spell doom for these kids" (p. 119). Even the casual observer will notice the difference in the conversations and casual language that kids use in school hallways and the conversations and formal language that fill effective classrooms. Academic literacy requires the development of robust formal language registers that should be practiced in all content-area classrooms. At school, language discourse patterns can be quite complex and abstract. Becoming proficient in these patterns will prepare everyone for future academic and career success.

Academic Language Registers

On the one hand, our students at school may be able to communicate informally with us and their peers, while on the other hand, they can lack the formal language and literacy skills to fully access the core content of school. Learning the academic language registers at school is in many ways like learning a second language. The casual language register is learned at home, and a second language register of academics is required at school. Henrichs (2006) notes, "One of the challenges that children face at school is to become proficient with the academic register. The academic register differs from the informal interactional register and is unfamiliar to many children as they start school" (p. 248).

For our English language learners, the academic language of school becomes the third language register they are expected to master. English language learners often acquire the speaking and listening aspect of a primary language register in their home. Within their first two years at school they usually acquire a casual English language register that allows them to negotiate the neighborhood, to socialize at lunchtime, and to speak with new friends. These students may use words imprecisely, conjugate verbs improperly, and structure language informally, yet still be understood by others. Haynes (2006) states, "Although English language learners may speak English on the playground, this does not mean they have mastered the academic and cognitive language of the classroom" (p. 24). Again, learning the academic language of school that leads to academic success is in many respects the second or third language register that our students need to learn.

In a variety of ways, academic language is more difficult to learn than other language registers, because it is so central to reading and writing. Many of our students only know how to speak and listen in the language registers of casual English. Academic language registers support academic discourse, and this discourse is most often centered within written text, journal articles, and content-area writing. Making the jump to the reading demands of formal expository text, story structure, and rigorous textbooks stretches the literacy abilities of many students (Feldman & Kinsella, 2005). Academic text is often abstract, and it introduces increasingly complex concepts. Developing the skills to write analytical essays, research papers, and academic reports creates another large gap that all too many of our students struggle to overcome. Academic language registers also support the creation of knowledge structures that help learners to become highly literate (Rosenshine, 1997), and when our schools effectively integrate the general academic language with the language of each specific content area, then our students will repeatedly and consistently have opportunities to engage in higher-level learning.

Professional Language Registers

As we think about various types of jobs in the workforce, we will find that nearly every profession has its own language register. Because different professions operate within different contexts, each profession develops a language register unique to its context and environment. Professional language registers differ in the words, discourse patterns, tools, and actions that must be developed to become proficient in a particular profession. When our students learn the academic language registers of different disciplines, this helps prepare them to learn the professional language registers of work. Simpson (2003) in his work contrasts the professional language register of culinary chefs with the professional language register of research biologists. Each profession has created its own terminology and precise language that helps people in that profession communicate effectively and do their jobs. Doctors, engineers, plumbers, attorneys, and mechanics all have their own language registers that are unique to their chosen profession.

In addition, each profession has its own professional discourse or specialized pattern for communicating. These professions have specific jargon or lingo, and knowing the language registers of these professions is important. Professional language registers support the professional discourse of a working community. Consider the following small sampling of professional language registers.

Types of Professional Language

- ***Builder*** (concrete foundation, roofing shingles, tiling, sheet rock, insulation, stucco, framing, etc.)
- ***Doctor*** (stethoscope, patient, femur, ventricle, scalpel, kidney stones, blood pressure, etc.)
- ***Auto Mechanic*** (transmission, piston, alternator, oil pan, spark plug, carburetor, etc.)
- ***Educator*** (pedagogy, schema, formative assessment, IEP, time-on-task, zone of proximal development, ADHD, etc.)

As professional language registers develop, they provide language to describe tools, concepts, processes, and actions that are associated with each profession. One of the purposes of this book is to contribute to the professional discourse and support the language of teaching and instruction. In many ways, academic language encompasses the skill and art of making the professional language register of instruction transparent for all of our students as they progress through school. Danielson (2007) observes that "Every profession establishes a language of practice, one that captures the important concepts and understandings shared by members of the profession" (p. 12). Learning the dynamics of academic language will help prepare us and our students for educational and professional success.

SOCIOECONOMIC BACKGROUND AND LITERACY

Education has been a critical key in helping many countries bridge the gap between the economic haves and have-nots. At the same time, in our own country, a gap seems to be widening between those that achieve academically and those that struggle and drop out. Research in the language patterns of young children has provided wonderful insights into the challenges so many of our students face as they strive to develop academic literacy. Hart and Risley (2003), over two and a half years, entered the homes of forty-two welfare, working-class, and professional families and patiently listened to the intimate conversations within the families. Their ambition was to record every interaction between the parents and their young children and determine the potential impact.

They listened intently to both the quality and quantity of these family conversations. They were surprised by what they found. After recording and compiling thousands of hours of conversations, they began to look at the language patterns that the adults used with their children in the home.

When Hart and Risley compared the three target groups, they observed that parents in professional homes communicated a much greater number of words and a greater variety of words than the parents in working-class homes. In turn, they also found that parents in working-class homes communicated a greater number of words and a greater variety of words than the parents in low-socioeconomic homes. In fact, their observations showed that high-socioeconomic three-year-olds understood over twice the number of words than their low-socioeconomic peers. At first, they questioned what this difference in language patterns might mean for these children and their future. They wondered how much the language differences observed at age three would affect individual learning and literacy at school. Would differences in the children's early experiences make a difference later in life?

Hart and Risley found that the language patterns manifest at age three significantly affected students as they prepared to enter school and as they proceeded through school. When they checked back in with the children six years later, their initial findings had become magnified. As we compare the plight of students from poor families with their wealthier peers, the research definitely highlights several dramatic differences. The gap in vocabularies begins before students enter school (see Table 3.1).

Table 3.1   Number of Words in Children's Vocabularies by Age Three

Children from welfare families	500 words
Children from working-class families	700 words
Children from professional families	1100 words

Source: Hart & Risley, 2003

Others have noticed similar disparities between students as they progress through school (Barton, 2003). The disparity initially finds its genesis in impoverished homes, yet the solution can be found in schools that attack the issue early and consistently to make up for the gaps in language, literacy, and learning.

The results of Hart and Risley's (2003) study were staggering in both the quantitative and qualitative impact home language has on children and their future experiences. Let's look at some of the numbers behind the research and what it may mean for many of our students. Simply, in quantity of words heard, the average child on welfare was receiving half as much language experience per hour compared to the average working-class child, and they heard less than one-third of the words compared to the average child in a professional family. Students from poverty enter school behind in both the quantity and quality of language needed to succeed in school. Consider the accumulative effects of the numbers in Table 3.2.

Table 3.2   Differences in Words Heard by Children by Socioeconomic Status

	Words Heard per Hour	Words Heard in a 100-Hour Week	Words Heard in a 5,200-Hour Year	Words Heard Over a 4-Year Period
Welfare	616	62,000	3 million	13 million
Working-class	1,251	125,000	6 million	26 million
Professional	2,153	215,000	11 million	45 million

Source: Hart & Risley, 2003

The research of Hart and Risley (2003) explained why this language gap existed and where it originated. They found that this language disparity correlates to differences in socioeconomic status. An alarming fact is that the differences grew wider, rather than diminished, as students progressed through school. After four years, a "30 million word gap" in the number of words heard in their homes existed between children in the lowest and highest socioeconomic groups.

In addition to communicating more frequently with their children, parents in professional homes tend to affirm their children with positive statements six times more than they express negative prohibitions. On the other hand, on average, welfare-class parents provide twice as many negative prohibitions as positive affirmations (see Table 3.3).

Table 3.3 Differences in Affirmations and Discouragements Heard by Children Each Year

Welfare homes	26,000 affirmations and 57,000 discouragements
Working-class homes	62,000 affirmations and 36,000 discouragements
Professional homes	166,000 affirmations and 26,000 discouragements

Source: Hart & Risley, 2003

Over time, children in welfare homes will hear twice as many negative comments from their parents compared to positive comments, while children in working-class homes will hear twice as many positive comments compared to negative comments. In professional homes, children will hear over six times more positive comments compared to negative comments, and the total number of words spoken is more than double the number of words communicated to a child in a welfare home. The consistent positive feedback also seemed to carry over into areas of social adjustment at school for these students, expressed in the form of higher expectations and personal aspirations. Tough (2008) summarizes Hart and Risley by noting, "They found that a child's experience of language mattered more than socioeconomic status, more than race, more than anything else they measured" (p. 43). Their research shows we need to encourage and engage our students in the language and literacy skills needed to overcome any poor hand they may have been dealt. Without explicit instruction and support, students who lack academic language and literacy will get further and further behind each year. By the time students hit third and fourth grade, when reading to learn becomes essential for keeping pace, the differences start to become ever more apparent.

Content-Area Literacy

As educators, we are keenly aware of the struggle that so many of our students encounter with the language found in textbooks and tests. Most of us know our schools face alarmingly high dropout rates, and students of poverty face even higher dropout rates. So, where do we find the solution? How do we stem the tide and reverse the effects that have been eroding the foundation of student success? The answer is firmly rooted in meeting both the language and literacy needs of our students in content-area subjects. Irvin, Meltzer, and Dukes (2007) note the importance of "helping students to become active participants in their quests to become competent, confident readers, writers, speakers, and thinkers requires classroom contexts that motivate and engage students coupled with explicit literacy instruction that supports the improvement of their skills" (p. 49). Without knowing the fundamental structure of language, a framework of literacy never materializes. All core-content teachers need to become teachers of literacy strategies. Heller and Greenleaf (2007) acknowledge that

> The best teachers of discipline-based literacy practices are themselves able to read, write, and think like scientists, historians, mathematicians, or specialists in other fields, and they are well aware of the specific challenges that people tend to face when learning to read and write in these ways for the first time. (p. 27)

Without academic language and the opportunity to develop academic literacy in every classroom, our students face restricted access to education and a growing exclusion from the primary activities that lead to achievement at school. Success in content-area classrooms requires that a framework of academic literacy be provided to each student.

Academic Literacy and Social Justice

The research shows that educational opportunity has been impacted by the linguistic disadvantages correlating to poverty, yet still educational opportunity and equity must be achieved. For students who are socioeconomically disadvantaged, academic literacy has become a critical issue, vital to the achievement of social justice. We find in our prisons that 60% of inmates are functionally illiterate, and 85% of adjudicated youth are also (Adams, 1990). Students who have been overlooked or dismissed because they lack the language registers required for school definitely need explicit classroom instruction to help them bridge the gaps in their understanding. Scarcella (2003) declares, "Learning academic English is probably one of the surest ways of attaining socioeconomic success in the United States today. Learners cannot function effectively in school settings without it" (p. 3). Social justice can be achieved if equal access to academic literacy is infused throughout each school classroom and developed within every student. The American dream of facing the land of opportunity confident and prepared to succeed is marred by the fact so many of our youth opt out of getting a diploma that serves as an admission ticket to future opportunities in college and career.

We need to systematically bridge this gap in social justice. Limited financial resources can impact students, yet limited language resources will create even larger long-term disadvantages for students. When linguistic limitations and disadvantages are met with an educator's expertise in academic language and literacy strategies, the results are academic success. Academic literacy develops the educational resources that become the social and economic capital for each student's future success. The answer, loud and clear, points toward a systematic inclusion of academic language instruction in all content areas and across the four modalities of academic literacy: listening, speaking, reading, and writing.

Access to Learning

Without academic language and the ability to engage in academic literacy, students face systemic exclusion from the primary learning practices of school. Their access to education and a bright economic future becomes restricted. Formal academic and professional language frequently serves as a gatekeeper for an individual's access to future opportunities. For many of our students who lack language and literacy, the physical doors of schools may be open, yet the doors of learning close ever tighter for them as they fall further and further behind. These students never seem to develop the literacy skills needed to read, speak, listen, and write at grade level. How do we give voice to our students who lack the literacy strategies and skills to succeed with academic textbooks, tasks, and tests? As teachers, are we concerned about our students' opportunities to have access to a viable economic future? An immediate concern for many of us is our students' ability to access the academic content of our classrooms. Our students who lack academic literacy also lack full access to subject matter content. Without the academic language and literacy skills to succeed in school, the dropout rate will remain around 30%, and it will be much higher for many of our students who come from poverty. Torgeson and colleagues (2007) state that "To meet the increasing literacy demands of the workplace, all students must leave high school capable of speaking and understanding academic English, reading complex texts for understanding, and writing expository texts with proficiency" (p. 94). Many students from poverty seem to feel destined for a lifetime of limited opportunities and economic disadvantage. Creating an equitable future for all students can happen as schools support the growth of academic language within each student and develop academic literacy in every classroom.

Academic Literacy and School

As an educational consultant, I have observed firsthand the importance of academic language and literacy for achieving success in elementary, middle, and high school. Our students need explicit strategies in each content area if they are to develop the literacy skills that can span the significant learning gaps that so many of our students currently face. Our schools need to make instruction in academic language and literacy a priority. As we provide instruction in academic literacy throughout each content area, we can positively impact achievement for all of our students. Content-area teachers in mathematics, science, social studies, and language arts note that many of their students lack many of the strategies and skills to succeed. Consider the following concerns:

- Do many of my students seem reluctant to read the assigned textbook?
- Do many of my students say they are listening to instructions yet have little idea what to do once assignments are started?
- Do many of my students avoid participating in class discussions about course content?
- Do many of my students say they complete reading assignments, yet they have little recollection of the content?
- Do many of my students say they have difficulty doing the assigned homework?
- Do many of my students seem to have little idea about constructing a cohesive paragraph?

Whether we teach a large number of socioeconomically disadvantaged students or we teach those who struggle with academic language, learning academic literacy strategies will make a significant difference for your students. Francis, Rivera, Lesaux, Kieffer, and Rivera, (2006) declare that "Mastery of academic language is arguably the single most important determinant of academic success for individual students" (p. 7). Explicit instruction should support literacy and language across content areas and prepare students to succeed academically now and in the future. Providing specifically targeted strategies to develop language and literacy skills will make a difference. Our students from poverty need more intensive language and literacy strategies (see Chapters 4 through 8) to help them bridge the gaps in their learning. With strategic instruction in each of the content areas, our students' chances for success will be greatly enhanced.

SUMMARY

Many students lack a foundation in academic language and an effective framework of academic literacy. Academic literacy is directly impacted by the level of academic language that learners develop, and academic achievement is directly impacted by the quality of academic literacy developed across content areas. It is imperative that students like George develop a proper foundation and create the framework, so they can do like Julie and build strategies for academic success in school. The academic language registers that our students develop in school will benefit both their academic and professional futures. Hart and Risley's (2003) research highlights the importance of providing all students, and particularly those from poverty, quality instruction in academic language and literacy. Our students who come to school with impoverished language definitely need a classroom rich in academic literacy to help bridge the language gaps they face before they even enter school. Social justice requires that we develop within all students the language skills and literacy strategies that will embrace educational access and increase student learning. Creating equitable opportunity means that we should do everything we can to scaffold a framework of literacy for every student who comes to our schools. Developing the reading, writing, listening, and speaking strategies associated with academic literacy will strengthen our students' abilities to succeed in school, in their careers, and beyond. In the upcoming chapters, we will dig into proven academic literacy strategies that will help you develop the academic language and skills for all students.

PERSONAL REFLECTIONS

1. How am I assisting all of my students to develop the literacy skills to achieve equity and receive the social justice they deserve?

2. In what ways do I explicitly provide students with instructional activities and strategies to help them develop a foundation and framework for content-area learning?

3. How do I expand the academic language registers of my students so they will develop their academic abilities and broaden their economic opportunities?

Academic Reading 4
Inferring Strategies

Language is the only instrument of science, and words are but the signs of ideas.

—Samuel Johnson

An essential part of learning is making important connections and developing effective comprehension. School is designed to help our students become aware of fundamental areas of study (mathematics, science, languages, social studies, arts, music, etc.), and it is designed to help them learn how to fill gaps in their understanding within these various subjects. Effectively negotiating these gaps in knowledge contributes to comprehension. When we are able to help our students bridge the gaps in their comprehension, the eventual result will be successful learning.

Jennifer's Story

Jennifer smiled from ear to ear with her white sparkling teeth showing her excitement. For the first time in her life, she'd finished a book without pictures. Jennifer had liked it even though she'd wondered if she would ever get through the entire book. The dreaded assignment from her social studies teacher had seemed like a terrible idea. Each student had to select a book about a historical figure and then write a two-page report. The book Jennifer reluctantly picked told the story of abolitionist Harriet Tubman. With over a hundred pages, it seemed like a huge obstacle. Jennifer was a seventh grader, yet she had avoided reading books even though she liked to learn. She began reading the book in class and found that even though she had difficulty with many words, it was amazing to learn about the Underground Railroad. It was terrific of Mrs. Anderson to patiently help her with some of the new words. Finishing the book felt like a huge accomplishment. The words had seemed so big and hard, and, honestly, at times she'd had difficulty understanding everything, yet she was able to figure most of it out and she did improve. Mrs. Anderson also demonstrated the structure of how stories are often written and this helped too. At times, Mrs. Anderson worked with Jennifer through each paragraph, and now Jennifer had earned an A- to show for it. She knew her mom would be so pleased. All of the hard work definitely seemed worthwhile. College seemed like it might fit into her future. Her success with reading and writing seemed to open the door of opportunity. Jennifer anticipated the hard work ahead and continued to smile at the possibilities.

READING COMPREHENSION AND THE "MATTHEW EFFECT"

An extensive base of research has determined that a lack of academic language directly affects reading comprehension. The National Reading Panel (2000) notes, "Comprehension is defined as 'intentional thinking during which meaning is constructed through interaction between the text and the reader.' Thus, readers derive meaning from the text when they engage in intentional problem-solving thinking processes" (p. 7). Academic language, academic comprehension, and academic learning share a mutually supportive relationship. This relationship has been called the "Matthew Effect" (Stanovich, 1993). The Matthew Effect refers to a parable of Jesus in the book of Matthew: "For whosoever hath, to him shall be given, and he shall have more abundance: but whosoever hath not, from him shall be taken away even that he hath" (King James Version, 13:12). The Matthew Effect notes that students who have large academic vocabularies are able to comprehend more successfully, and in turn this capacity to comprehend supports the learning of more academic language.

Unfortunately, the Matthew Effect also works in reverse. Students who struggle to read will gain less vocabulary, and smaller vocabularies make it more difficult to become a proficient reader. This is extremely troublesome news for socioeconomically disadvantaged students, who tend to enter school with significantly less academic language and smaller vocabularies. This language gap between students actually widens during school unless a concerted effort is made to reverse the effects. Table 4.1, adapted from Hirsch (2006) and Nagy and Anderson (1984), shows the comparison in the number of words learned each year by students from different socioeconomic groups.

Table 4.1 Words Learned Each Year

Reader Background	Estimated Words Learned per Year	Average Words Learned per Day
Socioeconomically disadvantaged students	3,000	7
Working-class students	5,000	12
Professional students	5,500	14

Juel (2008) states, "The more words children know, the more they will understand, learn from, and enjoy books and texts, as well as succeed on high stakes assessments" (p. 4). Students who know fewer academic language words struggle as readers. Vocabulary size generates a snowball effect as students progress through school. For students with large grade-level vocabularies, their snowball creates greater learning success. For students with small or below-grade-level vocabularies, their snowball creates greater frustration. Helping students avoid the negative downward spiral of the Matthew Effect and take advantage of the positive upward cycle created by increasing word knowledge in academic language is crucial to improving each student's level of comprehension.

DEVELOPING ACADEMIC READING SUCCESS

Reading success is highly influenced by the number and type of words that students know, because written text contains a significantly greater variety of words than everyday oral communication

(Cunningham & Stanovich, 1998). These authors also have noted that the language size of a student in the early grades provides a reliable predictor of academic performance in 11th grade. Our students who read regularly increase their academic vocabulary through inferring, and successful inferring increases their willingness to read. Schmoker (2001) notes, "It is worth emphasizing that the most important single activity to promote reading is reading. It is even better if this is done with a purpose, and if we regularly write about and discuss what we read" (p. 2). Up to 90% of the words students add to their vocabulary come from personal reading experiences outside of school. Table 4.2, from Anderson (1992), shows the number of minutes reading each day and its accumulated effects.

Table 4.2 Number of Minutes Reading

Percentile Rank	Minutes per Day		Words Read per Year	
	Books	Text	Books	Text
98	65.0	67.3	4,358,000	4,733,000
90	21.2	33.4	1,823,000	2,357,000
80	14.2	24.6	1,146,000	1,697,000
70	9.6	16.9	622,000	1,168,000
60	6.5	13.1	432,000	722,000
50	4.6	9.2	282,000	601,000
40	3.2	6.2	200,000	421,000
30	1.8	4.3	106,000	251,000
20	0.7	2.4	21,000	134,000
10	0.1	1.0	8,000	51,000
2	0.0	0.0	0	8,000

Source: Anderson, 1992

The quality as well as quantity of academic reading directly impacts students' academic success. For students who read infrequently, sustained silent reading in class can help, yet students need an arsenal of literacy strategies so they can read effectively in each content area. The best strategy for expanding our students' literacy is to help them become independent and confident readers. Successful readers engage in cognitive activities that are very different from struggling readers who have difficulty interacting effectively with text.

READING STRATEGY 1: COGNITIVE READING STRATEGIES

It is important to note, academic language skills should be learned as students develop cognitive reading strategies. Haynes (2006) states, "The research is clear that when teachers across content areas help students use reading comprehension strategies (such as summarizing, generating questions, and using semantic and graphic organizers), student learning improves substantially" (p. 4). The more cognitive reading strategies students know and use actively, the more successful they will be in comprehending text and truly learning. Torgeson and colleagues (2007) emphasize that cognitive strategies should be taught in each discipline: "Given the magnitude of the task adolescents face to be successful the growing consensus is that preparing all students . . . for academic reading tasks requires embedding literacy instruction in content-area classes" (p. 95). Research shows the sooner students engage with academic words, language, and knowledge structures, the better readers they will become (Pearson, Hiebert, & Kamil, 2007). Individually, cognitive reading strategies are effective; however, when these strategies are woven together in an overall approach, comprehension and learning greatly increases.

What Cognitive Reading Strategies Look Like

The following cognitive reading approaches will make a dramatic impact on struggling readers' ability to comprehend and learn.

- *Activate Prior Knowledge.* Prior knowledge serves as a lens we look through to understand new knowledge. Learning is successful when new information is linked to existing knowledge. The more prior knowledge students have in a particular content-area, the quicker they can absorb new knowledge and connect their learning to a network of understanding. Activating prior knowledge is like preparing soil, so that new seeds of knowledge can flourish. Students need to put their reading in context to make connections. Students appreciate when new information builds on what they already know.

- *Make Predictions.* Students can make predictions before they start reading by looking at the title, skimming pictures, and looking at headings to help give them an idea of what the contents may contain. Beers (2003) explains, "Skilled readers consciously try to anticipate what the text is about before they begin reading. They look at the cover, art, title, genre, author, headings, graphs, charts, length, print size, front flaps, and back covers. . . They do anything to find out something before they begin reading" (p. 74). Each time students read, they can make multiple predictions and reflect on what they have already read while anticipating future actions and information.

- *Build Background Information.* Background knowledge, schemata, and prior knowledge (or what is often called *concept knowledge)* all contribute to the ability to make more connections and to grasp deeper and more complex levels of meaning. Building background information begins with the language terms and concepts that are at the heart of the information. The more background knowledge an individual has to create connections to context, the more effective and efficient comprehension becomes.

- *Visualize.* Visualizing the colors, shapes, sizes, unique qualities, sounds, and signifying features help students learn. As students create mental images, they should consider the functions or actions that may occur as well as the characteristics of the situation. When the word *cat* is spoken, do your students see a cat clearly in their mind? What do they see the cat doing? Students need to be given opportunities to read rich writing that will help stimulate their ability to create vivid mental pictures.

- *Generate Questions.* Generating questions develops students' thinking and sparks their interest when they pose questions and anticipate answers. Questions help students focus and gives them something to consider. Asking questions of oneself causes reflection. The more students process the ideas in the text and their own ideas about the text, then the more they can learn. Students should be asked to generate questions before they read, while they are reading, and after reading.

- *Monitor Reading Comprehension.* Monitoring comprehension helps students direct their thinking processes and cognitive reading strategies toward successful meaning making and learning. Monitoring comprehension requires readers to look at larger passages of text as a whole, so the students can create a mental model of the material.

In addition to receiving a wide selection of cognitive activities in class, students need specific instruction in the strategies that make these activities work. Research by Rosenshine and Meister (1994) found that six to twelve lessons was an effective number of times that each cognitive reading strategy should be explicitly taught to students. Students who feel confident benefit from at least six lessons, while struggling readers benefit from twelve lessons or more that model cognitive reading strategies. Learning to develop cognitive reading strategies is a lot like learning how to become a good detective. In Table 4.3, consider the comparisons between detectives and investigators, and good readers (Wilhelm, 2001).

Table 4.3 Similarities Between Detectives and Good Readers

Detectives and Investigators	Readers
Ask questions	Interrogate authors and text
Use multiple sources of information	Build on their background knowledge
Predict and verify	Follow hunches about the author's direction and see if it is right
Monitor comprehension	Ask, "Does this text make sense? Is it leading me in a logical direction?"
Visualize	"See" stories by picturing them
Fill in unstated information	Try and find and add missing details
Assess reliability	Gauge whether an author's ideas are credible or whether they make sense given everything else that's going on in the story

Source: Adapted From Wilhelm, 2001

This analogy can be shared with your students to increase their understanding of several processes used in cognitive reading strategies.

How Cognitive Reading Strategies Work

These strategies work because the internal cognitive processes dictate how reading and comprehension develops as our students progress through school. Remember, the example lessons provided may need to be adapted for the specific content area and grade level of your students.

1. Provide a brief reading passage that activates students' prior knowledge in the content you are teaching for the day.

2. Ask students to make several predictions about the reading passage and what they think they will be learning for the day.

3. Provide background knowledge and guide students towards the connections between content concepts.

4. Invite students to describe how they picture the concepts covered with a peer in a quick pair-share.

5. Ask students to generate at least two questions for their partner and at least one extension question for themselves regarding the images they visualized.

6. Have students read another passage and ask them to monitor their reading and reflect on their learning.

7. Conclude with a class discussion about how they did in each of the seven cognitive strategies and whether they behaved like good detectives to discover the answers.

Planning at least six times each year when each of these cognitive reading strategies will be emphasized is important to improve reading comprehension and student learning.

READING STRATEGY 2: DEVELOPING INFERENCES

Students who develop a strong grasp of academic language become more successful at making inferences and making sense of text. Creating inferences is a meaning-making process that helps our students successfully negotiate gaps in their knowledge. The word *infer* is defined by Dictionary.com as the ability *to derive by reasoning; conclude or judge from premises or evidence*. As students develop their ability to infer effectively and efficiently, they will be able to create meaning from spoken discourse and written text. The ability to infer begins to develop long before kids even enter school. As toddlers, children observe the interactions surrounding them, and they are able to make connections between various relationships. Toddlers infer from their experiences and make connections about the world around them. As they overhear adult conversations, they make simple connections between spoken words and the relationship between the concepts conveyed by these words. Eventually words like *bottle, yum-yums,* or *more* begin to take on meaning as they become associated with food, and children begin to speak these words even though they may be mispronounced. Hirsch (2003) notes, "We learn from infancy that oral language comprehension requires readers to actively construct meaning by supplying missing knowledge and making inferences" (p. 17). Whenever students read text, it is particularly important that they engage in the inferential process so they can create meaning from the text (Hayes & Ahrens, 1988). Inferring meaning from the words and connections emphasized in text can help students comprehend the gist of the text. Inferences are often very subtle, and it is important for students to look at the context and the unwritten meaning conveyed by text.

What Developing Inferences Looks Like

Inferring is connecting our background knowledge to context clues contained in the text. The process of inferring is how our students learn the majority of new words. Students who learn to infer effectively find their comprehension and learning spiraling upwards. Making sure that every student understands both the process of inference and the important academic words for developing comprehension is critical to consistent learning success. A working definition of *inferring* could be described as: *using reason to construct meaning and bridge the gaps in our comprehension.* Consider the following statements and see if you are able to identify the inferences made:

"All men are mortal; Socrates will die some day."

These statements taken together expect the reader to make at least two inferences. The first notes that Socrates fits into the classification known as men. The second inference develops from knowing that being mortal has a causal connection to eventual death. Without the ability of the reader to make inferences in classification and causality, the communication process comes to a halt. If the ideas are explicitly stated in logical steps, the statement would read something like

"All men are mortal."

"Socrates is a man."

"Mortal beings die."

"Socrates will die someday."

If all communication was stated this explicitly, communicating would become truly tedious and redundancies would be all too frequent. Instead, whenever we express our ideas, we make certain implications. These implications make assumptions about our audience's level of prior knowledge and their ability to make connections. Finding the right balance between speaking concisely and being understood is part of the art of effective communication. Look over the following types of inferences and examples that highlight how inferences can be made.

Ways to Make Inferences

- **Infer Characteristics of an Object.** As they hauled the rust-encrusted chest off the ocean's sandy floor, they finally found inside what they had been seeking for so many months—we might infer gold or treasure is in the chest.
- **Infer Time.** The birds were singing on the newly budded branch as the sun surged above the horizon—we might infer it is a bright spring morning.
- **Infer Action.** With the stick flailing back and forth, the blindfolded third grader finally struck the torso and candy flew everywhere—we might infer the youth broke open a piñata.
- **Infer Location.** As the whistle blew, Tom waved goodbye and then made his way past the benches and lockers to the street—we might infer the individual is located at a train station.
- **Infer Feelings/Attitudes.** When the principal asked Jack to stand in front of the school and be recognized, his face got red—we might infer Jack was feeling embarrassed.
- **Infer Causal Relationships.** The huge cart rolled backwards over George's leg, and he was rushed to the emergency room—we might infer that George's leg was broken.

Providing explicit instruction in the inferential process is extremely important, particularly for disadvantaged or struggling students, because it is so crucial to students' ability to develop understanding and create meaning. Helping students infer meaning and make connections between important points of knowledge is part of the art and science of teaching (Marzano, 2007). When teachers share their thinking out loud, these subtle processes become more easily recognized and overt for students. As Wilhelm (2001) points out, students must learn inferencing skills to read all kinds of texts, not only narrative ones. And as this is a challenging skill to develop, it should be modeled for the students by the teacher.

How Developing Inferences Works

This strategy works because it helps students learn the cognitive processes that improve their ability to make connections.

Steps to Making Inferences

1. Analyze a reading selection carefully before presenting it to students. Identify three or four main ideas in the passage prior to assigning the reading selection to the class.

2. Develop a series of prereading questions for a planned reading assignment. Specifically, plan two questions for each main idea in the text. The first question should elicit previous knowledge of the topic. The second should point beyond previous knowledge and encourage students to imagine, speculate, and predict.

3. Have students write their predictions and speculations prior to reading the selection.

4. Again, before reading, encourage students to share both their prior knowledge of the topic and their predictions about the reading selection.

5. Next, ask the class to read the selection carefully. Be sure the students read the passage as a whole, without interruption.

6. After reading, have the students review their written predictions about the passage. Ask each student how the new information changed or reshaped his prior knowledge.

The following sentences can be used as a model exercise that will help students recognize the many inferences they can make as they read.

Sample Assignment for Developing Inferences

Read each sentence and make an inference about the possible characteristics, actions, relationships, and so on, and decide which types of inference each sentence exemplifies. After completing, please discuss your answers with a peer.

1. Bobby was the star quarterback, but he had a broken arm.
2. Someone shook the can of soda pop.
3. My quiz had fewer red marks than I expected.
4. Billy was called down to the main office.
5. George bought tickets and got Cindy some buttery popcorn.
6. We jumped in with a splash and enjoyed the experience tremendously.
7. Yesterday, after we cleaned out our desks, we had to take everything home.
8. Tommy blew out the candles and opened many gifts.
9. All of the numbers on my ticket matched the numbers in the newspaper.
10. I ran through the tape as I crossed the finish line.

Because the process of inferring is most often taken for granted, you will want to make transparent the thinking, inferring, and reasoning processes that your students engage in to become effective readers.

READING STRATEGY 3: CONTENT-AREA READ-ALOUDS

A content-area read-aloud is a wonderful strategy to help students construct meaning from text. Students enjoy listening to rich, well-written writing. Read-alouds provide struggling readers the opportunity to explicitly consider the inferences and cognitive processes used in reading. Read-alouds can convey important information in specific disciplines. When conducting a read-aloud, it is always a good idea for students to write down words that are unfamiliar or words they thought were particularly powerful. In addition to teacher read-alouds, students can also read to each other their own writing or the engaging, descriptive writing of professionals. At the conclusion of the read-aloud, academic words can be clarified in context, and students can share their favorite passages.

What Content-Area Read-Alouds Look Like

Content-area read-alouds bring the subject matter alive for students as they listen to real historians, scientists, mathematicians, and authors share insights into their crafts and subjects. These websites are excellent resources for finding rich content-area writing.

The following questions outline the types of questions that can engage your students during content-area read-alouds.

Content-Area Read-Aloud Resources

- Social Studies—http://history.com
- Mathematics—http://matharticles.com
- Science—http://sciencedaily.com
- Language Arts—http://mgfx.com/kidlit/

---

1. **Connecting.** Good readers connect their reading to things they already know.

   - Does this remind me of something?
   - Have I ever felt similar to this?
   - What do I already know that will help me understand this?
   - Has this ever happened to me before?
   - What other concepts do these ideas connect together?

2. **Predicting.** Good readers consider what may happen and make predictions based on what they know and what they have read.

   - Since this happened, I believe _____ will happen next.
   - I wonder how this will turn out.
   - What do I think will happen as a result of this?
   - As I look over the pictures and bold print, I anticipate I will learn about _____.

3. **Questioning.** Good readers continually ask themselves questions about their reading.

   - What do I feel the author is saying?
   - Who does this impact?
   - How does this fit in with the previous paragraph?
   - What does this mean for me?
   - Why is this happening?

4. **Monitoring.** Good readers pause and think about their understanding, and they reflect on what it means to them.

   - What have I learned so far?
   - Does this make sense?
   - Do I need to reread this past section?
   - What does this word mean?
   - What clues in the text will help me figure things out?

5. **Prioritizing.** Good readers recognize the most important information and can synthesize it in concise statements.

   - What are the main points of this passage?
   - How is the most significant information organized?
   - The author's most important ideas are . . .
   - What are the key academic words that cement the information together?
   - What are the key content-specific words and associated concepts?

6. **Visualizing.** Good readers create a picture of the things and concepts they are reading about.

- What pictures do I create in my mind while reading?
- What do I sense, hear, taste, smell, or feel as I read?
- Do I have a clear idea of how this information influences things?
- How do I visualize this information being organized in my mind?

Now, let's take a look at a read-aloud script you can share with your students to explain the reading process.

Sample Inferring Read-Aloud Script

Inferring is an important reading process for understanding or comprehending new information. Whenever I read a newspaper, instructions, or a book, I always anticipate the overall meaning the process asks me to understand. I look to get the gist or main message that the material I am reading is emphasizing. If I get distracted or lose concentration, I monitor my comprehension and go back and reread sentences or passages that I am still trying to understand. I slow down my reading or reread passages that have a lot of new words or important information. I also skim through certain information that is less important. Monitoring comprehension helps me recognize my ability to get the main idea or gist and to know when I need to slow down or quickly skim. I visualize or make a mental picture of what is happening when I read. The image I have constructed helps me see the situation and know how to connect any additional information or details. I monitor comprehension as I think about inferences and how I create meaning. I integrate this meaning within paragraphs or larger passages, and I make sure it makes sense to me. When I am monitoring reading comprehension, I can successfully adjust my approach to reading and learning. Now, let me read a two-page article; listen carefully as I model strategies for reading.

How Content-Area Read-Alouds Work

This strategy works because most students love to have someone read to them, particularly if it is rich, interesting information. Modeling read-alouds in class helps make the reading process more explicit for students as they learn to recognize reading strategies (Calderon, 2007).

- I'm going to visualize and think aloud about what I just read.
- I'm going to read chunks I can handle and then summarize.
- I'm going to change the title and subheadings into questions.
- I'm going to make predictions.
- What could that word mean? Let me reread.
- I'm going to stop and reread confusing parts of this sentence.
- I'm going to put a sticky note after this sentence so I can come back to it for clarification.
- What kind of test question would the teacher ask from this paragraph?
- How does this relate to the paragraph above?

Enjoy the read-aloud strategy, and have fun as you read exciting and interesting content to your students.

READING STRATEGY 4: INTEGRATING MULTIPLE INFERENCES

Creating meaning from a message requires inferring at three levels: the word level, the sentence level, and the text level. Inferring, in its simplest form, occurs primarily at the word level and within sentences. Integrating inferences is done within multiple sentences and paragraphs.

Monitoring inferences is done at the text level as students read a passage and become aware they are failing to make sense of the text. Connecting many of the dots and integrating multiple inferences contained within a passage becomes more important as middle school and high school texts become increasingly complex. Integrating inferences requires students to connect the context with the stated information in the text, and then connect this information with their prior knowledge. Students need to integrate inferences from the text as well as make inferences from prior knowledge or recently learned background information (Alfasi, 2004). A number of higher-order discourse skills contribute to the development of reading comprehension, including integrating multiple inferences and monitoring the meaning-making process. Cain and Oakhill (2007) note how important it is for students "to perform tasks such as inference, integration, and monitoring of comprehension, which are essential to building a representation of meaning" (p. 288). Integrating inferences and monitoring comprehension are strategies that help support understanding of academically complex and dense text.

What Integrating Multiple Inferences Looks Like

When proficient readers make multiple inferences as they read, the following types of learning occur (Keene & Zimmerman, 2007).

Readers

- Draw conclusions from text
- Make reasonable predictions as they read, then test and revise those predictions as they read further
- Create dynamic interpretations of text that they adapt while and after they read
- Use a combination of background knowledge and explicit information from the text to answer questions they have as they read
- Make connections between conclusions they draw and other beliefs or knowledge, and they use the inferences to extend and adapt existing knowledge
- Arrive at insight after struggling to understand complex concepts
- Make critical or analytical judgments about what they read

Students who successfully integrate multiple inferences into coherent meaning are able to more clearly develop comprehension and create stable knowledge structures. The *question-answer relationship* strategy works very well for developing multiple inferences.

How Integrating Multiple Inferences Works

The question-answer relationship (QAR) strategy works because it gets students to approach information from multiple perspectives. The QAR framework provides an effective model for helping students connect multiple inferences (Raphael, 1986). The QAR framework encourages students to consider four different types of perspectives across two broad categories: *in-the-book* (text-explicit) questions and *in-my-head* (text-implicit) questions. The in-the-book questions are generated directly when students are reading. These explicit questions fall into two subcategories: right-there questions found in a specific place in the text and think-and-search questions that are found by connecting different parts of the text to make inferences. The in-my-head questions are created by the reader when confronting a text. These questions are not explicitly found in the text; instead, these questions develop as the reader engages with text by reflecting and inferring. These implicit questions fit into two subcategories: author-and-you questions that the text cause the reader to consider and on-my-own questions where the reader connects information and ideas to prior knowledge and experiences (see Table 4.4).

Table 4.4 Types of QAR Questions

In the Book	In My Head
Right There The answer is easily found in the text. The exact words for the questions and answers are found in the same sentences.	*Author and You* The answers are outside of the text. The reader combines previous knowledge with text information to create a response.
Think and Search The answer is in the text but requires gathering information from different places in the selection.	*On My Own* The answers are outside of the text. The reader uses previous experience to respond.

STEPS TO QUESTION-ANSWER RELATIONSHIP INFERRING STRATEGY

1. Provide a reading selection and a set of questions about its content.

2. Explain the two broad categories of questions (and the four subcategories) to students as an introduction to the QAR strategy.

3. Model the placement of the questions in the framework of the QAR model.

4. Next, divide the class into small groups and provide each with a reading selection and a set of questions. Have the groups sort questions based on the QAR framework.

5. Finally, provide the groups with a new reading selection and ask them to develop questions from its content. Have the students evaluate their own questions in light of the QAR framework.

Right-here questions are typical of the types of question found in the back of textbooks that are answered very easily. Think-and-search questions help students recognize text patterns (e.g., compare/contrast, description, time-order, or cause-effect) as they pull examples from throughout the text. Author-and-you questions help students connect to the text. On-my-own questions encourage students to connect to prior knowledge and the world around us.

ACADEMIC READING CHALLENGE

Let's see if you are ready for a fairly difficult academic challenge. Consider the following question: *What percentage of words need to be included in a reading passage for most students to be able to infer successfully?* Please write down your answer here: _____.

Whenever I ask this question at an educational conference or professional development seminar, I get a variety of responses. The answers have ranged from 5% to 99%, yet most of the answers fit somewhere between 50% and 90%. What did you determine? Rather than tell you the answer to the above question, experience the challenge for yourself, and see how it goes. See if you can successfully infer the meaning of the missing words and effectively comprehend the passage in Figure 4.1.

Figure 4.1 Reading Challenge I

_____ is critically _____ to the _____ of children's _____ skills and therefore to _____ ability to _____ _____ education. Indeed, _____ has come to _____ the "essence of _____" (Durkin, 1993), _____ not only_____ academic _____ in all subject _____ but to _____ _____ as well. In carrying out its _____ of the extant _____ in reading _____, the NRP _____ three predominant _____ in the research on the _____ of _____ comprehension skills. First, _____ _____ is a complex cognitive _____ that cannot be understood _____ a clear description _____ the _____ that _____ development and _____ _____ play in the understanding _____ what has been _____. Second, _____ is an active _____ that _____ an intentional and thoughtful interaction _____ the _____ and the text. _____, the preparation of _____ to better _____ students to develop _____ apply _____ comprehension _____ to enhance _____ is intimately linked _____ students' achievement in this _____. Because these three _____ serve as the _____ for _____ how best to help _____ develop _____ comprehension abilities, the extant _____ relevant to vocabulary _____, to text _____ instruction, and to _____ preparation of _____ to teach reading comprehension _____ was _____ in detail _____ the NRP.

How did it go? The previous passage contains 70% of the words. Most adults still struggle significantly as they strive to infer meaning from this passage. Even though 70% of the words are included, this passage is very difficult to read and comprehend. The previous passage came from the National Reading Panel's (2000) report, and it emphasizes explicit instruction and reading comprehension. Even though the report addresses a couple of issues that we have been discussing, the missing words make it very difficult for the reader to understand. It requires knowledge of much more than 70% of the language terms for quality inferring and comprehension to occur. How about another challenge? If you are up for it, read another passage (Figure 4.2) from the Reading Panel's Report, with fewer words missing, and see how it goes.

Figure 4.2 Reading Challenge II

Teaching _____ comprehension strategies to students at all grade levels is complex. Teachers not only _____ have a firm grasp of the content _____ in text but also must have substantial knowledge of the strategies themselves, of which _____ are most effective for different students and types of _____ and of how best to _____ and model strategy use. Research on comprehension strategies has _____ dramatically over the last two _____. Initially, investigators focused on teaching one strategy at a time; later studies examined the effectiveness of teaching _____ strategies in combination. However, implementation of this promising _____ has been problematic. Teachers _____ be skillful in their instruction and be able to respond flexibly and _____ to students' needs for instructive feedback as they read.

With at least 90% of the words provided, the text becomes much easier to read. Most individuals can infer meaning from the text, even though 10% of the words are missing from the passage. Some readers may want to go back and reread the passage to strengthen their understanding, yet knowing 90% of the words in the passage can help readers do a good job of inferring and creating meaning from the text.

READING STRATEGY 5: THE 90% RULE OF COMPREHENSION

Research in comprehension has determined the optimum level of background language for supporting student learning while also increasing the student's literacy development. When students know 90% of the vocabulary words used in a reading passage, they are able to infer successfully and generate meaning (Stahl, 1999). In addition, knowing 90% of the words helps the reader to use context clues, cognitive strategies, and inferring abilities that strengthen reading comprehension and also support learning additional words (Nation, 1990). The 90% rule is extremely important in our discussion regarding socioeconomically disadvantaged students. If students only know 70% of the words in a particular passage, they will be unable to infer effectively, and they will quickly come face to face with frustration. If a student's academic language fails to keep within at least 90% of the academic rigors of classroom texts, then eventually students will feel overwhelmed, and a loss of motivation is almost surely to occur. So, what can be done to assist a growing number of frustrated students? The answer lies in meeting the language demands of text by supporting students' gaps in word knowledge. Just as monitoring comprehension helps students infer meaning from text, teachers need to monitor students' language comprehension to make sure all students know at least 90% of the words before they are asked to engage in reading and comprehending the text (Rog, 2003).

What the 90% Comprehension Rule Looks Like

- *Frustration Reading Level.* (below 90% Comprehension)
- *Instructional Reading Level.* (90%–95% Comprehension range)
- *Independent Reading Level.* (95% Comprehension or higher)

Reversing the Trend

Content-area teachers can begin to bridge the achievement gap by insuring that every student's word knowledge is up to the 90% level of comprehension. As struggling students learn how to appropriately predict, question, infer, and use cognitive strategies, they will experience a liberating ability to increase their capacity to learn. Hirsch (2006) declares that the language gap can be decreased:

> If a student who is behind in word knowledge can be brought to know 90% of the words that she hears and reads in school, then she can pick up new words at a faster rate than the advantaged student who already knows 95% of the words heard and read in school.

Many of the schools that I consult have large numbers of socioeconomically disadvantaged and often no-advantaged students. It is amazing to see the results the teachers achieve by focusing on the 90% rule of comprehension, which states that all students need to know at least 90% of the academic words in each lesson so they can infer meaning.

How the 90% Comprehension Rule Works

This strategy works because most of the new words that students add to their growing vocabulary are learned from their reading experiences. In fact, approximately 90% of the words students learn in a given year are gained when they infer meaning from their reading (Stanovich, 1993).

1. Explicitly teach students key academic language (see Chapter 6 for a wonderful and easy-to-follow method).

2. Explicitly teach students specific content language.

3. Make sure students know and use multiple ways to infer meaning.

4. Encourage students to read outside of school and report on their reading.

Once students receive explicit instruction in academic language, they are on their way to effective inferring and efficient comprehending. By the 12th grade, it is estimated that the average student has learned roughly 60,000 to 100,000 words over their years before and during school (Hirsch, 2006). Teachers can then help their students recognize how academic language can lead to successful academic reading, which in turn produces academic literacy and achievement.

READING STRATEGY 6: THE 95% RULE FOR FLUENCY

Just as 90% word recognition is the magic level for students to comprehend reading material and create meaning, the 95% level is optimal for developing fluency and supporting the acquisition of more language into their vocabularies. "Thus the concept of independent reading level is important: it is the level at which the child recognizes more than 95% of the words and can read without laboring over decoding" (Learning First Alliance, 2000, p. 5). For example, when students with only an 80% grasp of the language are asked to read in class, you may find they struggle to read at a normal rate with expression, intonation, and inflection. On the other hand, students who have a 95% or greater grasp of the language should be able to read at a normal rate and add appropriate expression, intonation, and inflection. Fluently reading text, particularly the textbooks of the classroom, and developing clear comprehension, creates confidence and motivation in readers.

What The 95% Fluency Rule Looks Like

Developing reading fluency leads to successful reading confidence, while a lack of fluency leads to frustration. Students who can read 95% of the words in a passage are able to read fluently.

Reading Fluency

- Appropriate rate or speed
- Accuracy in processing
- Proper intonation and inflection

Students who have frequent experiences where they successfully comprehend text have a greater desire to read more.

How the 95% Fluency Rule Works

1. Teachers share what type of reading they do for enjoyment.

2. Students independently use previously learned reading strategies.

3. Students reread to a partner to practice fluency and develop shared comprehension.

4. Students reread class material chorally to build confidence.

Fluent readers enjoy reading more frequently and for longer periods of time. Outside-of-class reading improves word knowledge, and knowledge of words and language increase reading fluency. The majority of the words learned each day, about 90%, are acquired because of the out-of-class reading that students do. This mutually reinforcing cycle of increasing word knowledge and improving reading fluency demonstrates the direct benefits that frequent fluent reading can have on student learning.

READING STRATEGY 7: METACOGNITIVE MONITORING

Cognition means "to think" and a working definition of metacognition is "thinking about our thinking." Monitoring our comprehension and evaluating the inferences we make is a metacognitive process. Taylor and Pearson (2002) state that "capable thinkers know when and where to use the [cognitive reading] strategies they have acquired because they possess extensive meta-cognition about strategies, knowledge about the contextual appropriateness of strategies which has largely developed from actual use of strategies" (p. 401). Metacognition helps learners focus their attention and energy on the purposes of their reading. Providing students with a purpose gives them a direction in which to focus. Perkins-Gough (2002) found that rereading expository text with a purpose is a powerful strategy for promoting both fluency and deep understanding in every discipline. When teachers provide students multiple opportunities to engage metacognitively with a passage of text, the students develop greater comprehension and confidence in their abilities as readers.

What Metacognitive Monitoring Looks Like

Metacognition helps students monitor their ability to make meaning and apply strategies that will improve comprehension. The top five metacognitive or monitoring processes that improve students' comprehension (adapted from Sheorey & Mokhtari, 2001) follow.

Metacognitive Monitoring

- I try to get back on track when I lose concentration. (Students attend to overall meaning.)
- When text becomes difficult, I pay closer attention to what I am reading. (Students focus on comprehension.)
- When text becomes difficult, I reread it to increase my understanding. (Students monitor their level of comprehension.)
- I adjust my reading speed according to what I am reading. (Students read slower for more complex and dense text.)
- I think about what I know to help me understand what I read. (Students connect a text's message to their prior knowledge.)

How Metacognitive Monitoring Works

The following steps (adapted from Harvey & Goudvis, 2007) are effective for helping students monitor their comprehension metacognitively.

1. Help your students become aware of their thinking as they read.

2. Monitor their thinking and understanding, and keep track of meaning.

3. Ask them to listen to the voice in their head to make sense of text.

4. Notice when they stray from thinking about the text.

5. Notice when meaning breaks down.

6. Detect obstacles and confusions that derail understanding.

7. Understand how a variety of strategies can help them repair meaning when it breaks down.

8. Know when, why, and how to apply specific strategies to maintain and further understanding.

9. Reconstruct meaning or an overall gist.

10. Review the concepts in the passage multiple times.

11. Recheck for context clues in the reading.

Student comprehension and learning will improve as we clearly model for our students multiple strategies to engage in reading.

SUMMARY

Learning to make inferences and create meaning will open up worlds of understanding for students like Jennifer, as well as millions of other struggling readers. Because of the snowballing aspect of the Matthew Effect, students with less academic language and fewer literacy strategies get further behind their peers as they progress through the grades unless they receive explicit, strategic support. Content-area teachers can greatly reduce language gaps, literacy gaps, and the gaps in student achievement by teaching cognitive reading strategies and putting students in a position to infer effectively. Teachers need to teach strategies that help students develop multiple inferences, generate questions, predict, develop background knowledge, monitor reading, visualize, and think metacognitively. When students know 90% of what they are expected to read in an assigned reading passage, inferring engages at productive levels, creating a positive learning effect. When both the general academic language and specific content language are explicitly developed, students can engage in the process of inferring, thereby generating the bulk of new words added to their vocabularies and new learning. Students who know 95% of words in a passage are able to read fluently and independently while maintaining comprehension. Every classroom has students who need scaffolded strategies to develop fundamental literacy skills and academic language. Supporting the intertwining relationship between reading comprehension, academic language, and learning will help students develop effective academic literacy.

REFLECTIONS

1. How do you ensure that all students know 90% of the words in their reading assignments?

2. Which cognitive reading strategies do your students know and use regularly?

3. How often do you provide content-area read-alouds to engage your students and improve their understanding and thinking?

5 Academic Text Structure

For All these have students create their own!

Reading comprehension is thinking guided by print.

—Charles A. Perfetti, cognitive researcher

For every child, the ability to read text and comprehend language is a basic hallmark of literacy. Most of the texts our students face in academic settings are organized into predictable, recognizable patterns. These patterns are structured to convey concepts and ideas in an orderly fashion. Written text typically follows a more formal pattern than verbal communication. Recognizing the patterns that organize text is important for improving reading comprehension. Because readers are unable to directly ask clarifying questions of the authors, identifying the structural patterns of texts can help them organize important information and develop deeper comprehension. When our students read text, they experience patterns that have been well established in writing for centuries. Knowing the common patterns used to organize text will help our students develop as both readers and writers. The words, phrases, and language structures included in text patterns are revealed to our students through academic language.

Kim's Story

Kim loves listening to Mrs. Jorgeson read to her class on the rug. Sitting with legs crossed, the time on the rug is special, with pictures and new words that express new ideas and feelings. Her heart always jumps at story time. It seems Mrs. Jorgeson makes the characters come alive, and Kim can almost picture herself in the story. Yet, something seems to happen as Kim leaves Mrs. Jorgeson's class and proceeds through the elementary years. As she has to face the academic challenges of reading textbooks alone in middle school, reading becomes a very different experience. Suddenly, Kim feels lost and confused as she reads classroom assignments. She searches for a way to better understand and enjoy reading.

ACADEMIC LANGUAGE AND ACADEMIC TEXT STRUCTURE

Academic language contains the words that help us to identify common text structures. As students progress through their academic careers, they will face an ever-increasing amount of text to read. Negotiating this increasing text demand begins in elementary school, ramps up in middle school, and then really takes off as students enter high school. High school students are often expected to read over a million words of text a year (Hiebert & Kamil, 2005). For juniors and seniors planning to attend college, the expectation quickly rises to a minimum of two million words of text a year. Much of this reading is done in ever-thicker textbooks that are striving to pack all of the state standards into a comprehensive curriculum. Students are expected to read a variety of texts as they progress through school. Knowing how to approach the text so that the academic language demands are appropriately met can be a major challenge for many students. Students who understand the structures of written text are able to keep up with the literacy demands of school. Academic language is a critical part of recognizing various types of text structure, and academic language helps students unlock the conceptual complexity of these text structures.

The types of academic language that reveal text structures are transition words. Transition words help signal to the reader the upcoming important passages, and they help the reader identify key concepts contained in the text. For example, transition words like *once upon a time, since, to begin with, for example, consequently,* and *finally* help the reader see shifts in the direction the text takes, and they can help the reader anticipate upcoming information. Transition words like *if . . . then, because, therefore, nevertheless, due to, for this reason, consequently, as a result,* and *thus* help glue important concepts together for the reader. Dickson, Simmons, and Kame'enui (1995) put it this way, "Text structure and student awareness of text structure are highly related to reading comprehension. Explicit instruction in text presentation and structures facilitates comprehension" (p. 2). Students who can anticipate the transition words in text and recognize related ideas are better able to negotiate the meaning of written text, and they are better able to comprehend the various types of text they are invited to read.

HOW DO WE IMPROVE STUDENT COMPREHENSION?

increase in academic language
knowledge of text structures
so does reading comp

Comprehending text may be the number one factor that leads to success in school. When students comprehend the material that is being covered, they are able to use this understanding to develop knowledge structures that can create further meaning. The process of *instruction* is about developing *internal structures* and creating meaning from those structures. Being aware of text structures helps students create their own knowledge structures and generate meaning from the text. Snow (2002) describes reading comprehension as "The process of simultaneously extracting and constructing meaning through interaction and involvement with written language" (p. 11). As students' knowledge of academic language increases and their knowledge of text structure increases, so does their reading comprehension.

Reading in school typically includes two areas of skill development for improving reading comprehension: reader-based factors and text-based factors. As readers engage with the structure of the text, then they can better understand the purposes of the passage and deepen their understanding. In addition to the reader-based and text-based factors, reading comprehension increases as the reader considers the methods authors use to construct text. Readers

Reader Response
+
Text-based

bring certain skills to the table that enable them to cognitively process assigned reading material. The text also places certain cognitive demands on the reader. Finding a nice fit between the reader-based skills and text-based demands is an important part of supporting successful reading comprehension. Table 5.1 outlines key reader-based and text-based factors that impact reading comprehension.

Table 5.1 Developing Reading Comprehension

Reader-Based Factors	Text-Based Factors
• Awareness of sounds • Letter-Sound relationships or decoding ability • Fluency or speed and accuracy • Comprehension strategies used by the reader • Knowledge of academic language and content-specific language • Prior knowledge and interest	• Structure of text • Narrative versus expository text • Quality and richness of language used in the text • Density and difficulty of academic language and concepts • The author's purpose and intent

The relationship that develops between the reader and the text is important in developing comprehension. When reader-based factors and text-based factors are effectively combined with an understanding of the author's intent and the reader's purpose for interacting with the text, then the reader can generate meaningful learning.

EXPLICIT INSTRUCTION AND TEXT ANALYSIS

Explicit instruction in the structure of academic text will help all students. It is important to explicitly teach academic language that both identifies text structure and supports the comprehension of meaning within the text. Students, particularly those who struggle with reading, should be explicitly taught how to identify the different types of text structures used in various textbooks, stories, and expository writing. Stahl and Nagy (2005) note it is important that "the teacher directs the children's attention to text structure and language structure" (p. 220). Students should be explicitly taught how to recognize the academic language signals that serve as clues for determining different types of story patterns and text structures. Students can use academic language as a key to unlock the patterns that are commonly used to organize different text structures. Learning First Alliance (2000) identifies several methods for improving instruction: "Engaging children in text comprehension may occur before, during, and after reading a text. From kindergarten onward, specific comprehension strategies can be explicitly taught" (p. 8). Explicit instruction in text structures should include the following three methods (adapted from Roit, 2006):

1. Explicitly discuss different types of texts (text structures).

2. Teach linguistic clues to identify text structures (signal words).

3. Organize and generate quality writing (modeling writing is discussed in Chapter 8).

Most students need explicit instruction in the several types of text structures. When students learn the academic language that signals these text structures, they will be better prepared to keep up with the increasing academic demands of school.

TEXT STRATEGY 1: CONTRASTING NARRATIVE AND INFORMATIVE TEXT

Story based

The books and passages commonly read in school fit into two main categories: narrative text and expository or informative text. Academic language is very important as readers strive to identify the text-based demands of various narrative and expository texts. On the one hand, *narrative text* refers to the literary format that is common in the primary grades of elementary school and is most often story based. Narrative or story-based text includes the books many parents read to their children even before school begins. Story-based text helps students learn about characters both fictional and nonfictional and about the variety of experiences the characters may face. Knowing the structure of story-based literature and the aspects of varying genres can help students remember the information in the stories (Olson & Gee, 1991).

On the other hand, *informative text* refers to the organizational format that is common in textbooks. Kame'enui and Carnine (1998) state, "In textbooks and other expository texts, organizational features and structures help students understand, learn from, and remember what they read. Research has shown that understanding how text is organized helps readers construct meaning" (p. 28). Identifying and understanding the various types of text structure helps students to "read between the lines" and "identify the signals" that are vital to academic comprehension.

What Comparing Narrative and Informative Text Looks Like

Text structure can be organized in a variety of ways, yet the two primary formats for organizing text are narrative and informative. Students often need help as they transition to middle school and high school, where most reading becomes information based. Let's consider the comparisons of narrative and informative text in Table 5.2 (adapted from Snow, Griffin, & Burns, 2005).

Table 5.2 Narrative and Informative Text — *Show kids this or build w/ them*

Narrative Text	Informative Text
Character-oriented toward the actions of a particular character	*Subject-oriented* towards a particular topic or issue
Primary purpose: *to entertain* and to provide a literary or aesthetic experience	Primary purpose: *to explain*, to present information, or to persuade
Based on *life experiences* and relationship between characters	Based on *abstract concepts* and relationship between ideas
Academic language may be less essential with few new words introduced; often contains *dialogue* and many words common in spoken language	*Academic language* is essential to comprehension; introduces many content-specific words and complex sentence structures
Most often employs a predictable sequenced pattern along a timeline; conveys a *beginning, middle,* and *end* of events	Uses a *variety of text patterns:* compare and contrast, description, cause and effect, problem and solution, chronological sequencing
Links the character's actions or a sequence of events in time-order, beginning, middle, and end	*Links relationships* between ideas from most important idea to supporting ideas with examples
Has *illustrations* that show actions of characters	Has *charts, diagrams, pictures,* and/or *tables*
Reader questions: Who is the main character? What happened next? How did the problem get solved?	Reader questions: What is the main subject? What are the supporting details? How can I use this information?

Source: Adapted from Snow, Griffin, & Burns, 2005

How Comparing Narrative and Informative Text Works

The following strategy works as students recognize the variety of patterns that highlight the challenges of informative text.

1. Place students in various groups with three or four members in each group. Ask each member of the group to read two passages (one passage should be a short story and the other a passage of informative text).

2. After students finish reading the two passages, ask them to discuss which text is a story and which text is informative, and direct them to determine what factors reveal the difference.

3. Have students complete a Venn diagram to outline the differences, with cited examples, while also noting any similarities in the middle section.

4. Invite students to share their results as a group with the entire class. The repeated exposure and examples will help students recognize the difference and start to appreciate the aspects of informative text.

5. Provide students with an outline to consider and review every time they read informative text in class.

   - What is the key subject in this passage of text?
   - What is the primary purpose of this passage of text?
   - What are the main concepts in this passage of text?
   - List some of the key academic language in the text?
   - How is the text pattern organized? (See Strategy 2 for help.)
   - What connections can you make about the information in the text?
   - What charts or other resources help you understand the text?
   - What questions did you generate or ask as you read the text?

6. Ask students to review the outline before they prepare for quizzes or tests.

[handwritten margin note: Good way to compare Narrative + Text Based Informative]

TEXT STRATEGY 2: RECOGNIZING STORY PATTERNS

Story structure analysis is also referred to in many educational circles as *story grammar.* Story grammar helps students improve their reading comprehension by giving them a framework they can use as they read stories. Story grammar addresses the structural elements of a story, including setting and characters, goals, challenges, action and efforts, consequences, and concluding reactions or solutions. Research shows that understanding the key components of story grammar helps students more easily understand key elements of the story and more effectively retain the information for future use (Beck & McKeown, 2004). Story grammar contains the basic framework of the story; it provides structure and the main idea of the story that the supporting details are built around.

What Story Patterns Look Like

The ability of readers to analyze and understand story structure or story grammar helps them outline the patterns or sequences of events of stories.

Parts of the Story Grammar Pattern

- Setting and characters
- Goals
- Challenges faced
- Actions and efforts
- Consequences
- Concluding actions or solutions

The triangle ∧

As students effectively anticipate the future events in stories, personal interest can build and comprehension can increase. The structure of story grammar allows readers to recognize a common framework or genre and then organize information into the framework as they create their own personal meaning.

Teacher	Okay, let's stop for a second and think aloud about several different kinds of story genres and which genre we may be reading. Raise your hands and tell me some of the different story genres, and I will write them on the board.
Students	Fantasy. Realistic Fiction. Folk Tale. Mysteries. Adventure.
Teacher	Terrific! Let's consider what you have noticed so far in the story to see if we can identify the story's genre? Let's do a quick think-pair-share. As you prepare your thoughts, please frame your answer with the following structured sentence frame written on the board: "I recognized at least three items of interest: _____, _____, and _____. These items helped me identify the story as _____ genre." Think about the question for 15 seconds and then turn to your partner and each share your answers for 45 seconds. Remember, I will call on three students to share with the entire class.
Students	(Engaging discussion and peer-to-peer interaction for two minutes.)
Teacher	Hey, I overheard some great dialogue and insights. Billy, please stand and use the sentence frame to fill in the answers for the first statement.
Billy	I recognized at least three items of interest: a crazy wizard who casts spells, a dwarf with a battle axe, and a really ugly troll.
Teacher	Thank you . . . Whitney, would you like to share next?
Whitney	I recognized at least three items of interest: a princess looking for prince charming, an enchanted castle, and a beautiful horse.
Teacher	Very nice . . . Carlos, will you please provide your answers to both statements?
Carlos	I recognized at least three items of interest: a gnome, a scary forest, and the castle. These items helped identify the story as a fairy tale genre.
Teacher	Correct . . . How many had fairy tale as the answer for the second statement? Fantastic! Okay, let's read on in our story.

Students who have limited experience with stories because of their family situation and students with learning disabilities definitely benefit from explicit instruction in story grammar and identification of story genre.

How Story Patterns Work

1. Tell students they are going to read a story (pick an appropriate storybook) and learn how to become better readers.

2. Read the title and show pictures while helping students identify the story genre (fantasy, mystery, folk tales, adventure, realistic fiction, etc.).

3. Read about the setting and characters.

4. Ask students to make a prediction about the goals of the characters and the potential challenges they may face.

5. Have students answer the 5 W's of *who, what, where, when,* and *why?*

6. Invite students to predict the actions and consequences that will unfold in the story.

7. When finished with the book, ask students to evaluate the decisions the characters made throughout the story.

Although story grammar applies primarily to stories in the elementary grades, story patterns also work at the secondary level with the conflict-plot pattern and a variety of genres (drama, biography, comedy, science fiction, mythology, satire, poetry, historical, etc.). Since our students may struggle to keep pace with the daily linguistic demands of today's texts as they are asked to transition from fewer narrative stories to more informative texts, we should make sure all students understand the structure of the underlying text.

TEXT STRATEGY 3: RECOGNIZING INFORMATIONAL TEXT STRUCTURE

A common characteristic of informative or expository text is the consistent use of text structures. Understanding informative text structure is important for our students, as this type of text is a staple of the upper grades in elementary school, middle school, and high school. Text structure increases in complexity the further students go in their education. The sooner students can identify the types of text structures and recognize the organization of concepts contained in text, the sooner they will be able to effectively retain the material and comprehend key concepts. Honig, Diamond, and Gutlohn (2000) note that

> As students progress through school, they devote most of their reading time to expository texts. In each new piece of expository text, readers face the challenge of uncovering its organization pattern—understanding the presentation, relationship, and hierarchy of ideas. Reading and understanding expository text involves more abstract thinking than does reading and understanding the typical narrative. Students need to compare and contrast ideas, recognize complex causality, synthesize information, and evaluate solutions proposed for problems. (p. 35)

The more efficient students become at identifying text structure, the more effective they will be at organizing ideas, and the more successful they will be academically. Let's take a look at the four most prevalent types of informative text structure.

What Informational Text Structures Look Like

The complexity of text increases as students progress through school, and greater text complexity increases the difficulty level of comprehension for readers (Beier & Ackerman, 2005). As the complexity of text increases in school, the importance of developing academic language also increases. Academic language is used both to identify key concepts in the text and to construct expository text. Text structure is often defined as the semantic and syntactic organizational tools used to convey concepts in writing (Rose, 2004). The semantic aspect of text structure includes the academic language and vocabulary words used to convey meaning. The syntactic aspect of text structure includes the way language is organized to support meaning. Academic language helps students identify the text structure, and it helps to scaffold the academic demands of the text. Students who have developed their knowledge of text structures and the academic language that signals types of text structure can dramatically improve both their reading and writing skills. The following list outlines the standard text structures used in most expository articles and textbooks:

Types of Informational Text Structures

- Cause-Effect or Problem-Solution
- Compare/Contrast
- Description or Explanation
- Sequencing or Time-Order

How Informational Text Structures Work

We all look for signals or cues to confirm for us that we are on the right track. When students learn the signals of expository text and how the text is constructed, then they will be more prepared to anticipate, predict, and process the material that is being presented. Comprehension increases significantly when learners explicitly understand the fashion in which text is organized, and they know the signals that reveal the order of the text. Meyer (2003) notes that "Research shows that signaling the organization of text or signaling main ideas yields superior recall of main ideas" (p. 214). Signal words are key academic language terms that identify various types of text structure. Table 5.3 (adapted from Honig et al., 2000) outlines several important text structures and the signal words that alert the reader to upcoming patterns for organizing information in the text.

Table 5.3 Text Structures and Their Signal Words and Meanings

Text Structure	Signal Words (*Good Chart*)	Message to Reader
Cause/Effect or Problem-Solution	Because, due to, since, therefore, so, as a result, consequently, nonetheless, if . . . then, accordingly, thus, nevertheless	These signal words alert the reader to cause(s) leading to effect(s), or problem(s) leading to solution(s).
Compare and Contrast	Like, just as, similar, both, also, too, unlike, different, but, in contrast, on the other hand, although, yet, either . . . or, however, while, as well as, not only . . . but also, comparatively, likewise, instead	The signal words alert the reader to upcoming comparisons and contrasts.
Description or Explanation	Moreover, as with most, additionally, in other words, furthermore, second, next, then, finally, most important, also, in fact, significantly, imagine that, for instance, particularly, for example, in front, beside, near	These signal words alert the reader to an upcoming list or set of characteristics.
Sequencing or Time-Order	Before, eventually, first, during, while, as, frequently, at the same time, after, initially, whenever, secondly, then, next, at last, finally, now, recently, when, to begin with	The signal words alert the reader to a sequence of events, actions, or steps.

The following steps will help students learn various text structures as they read content-area information (adapted from Readance, Bean, & Baldwin, 2004). This activity should be done at least four times on different weeks to go over each of the four text patterns.

Text Structure Activity

1. Explain the types of text structure patterns, and provide a simple example of each type.

2. Invite readers to brainstorm their own list of potential transition signal words that can provide clues to text structure patterns.

3. Ask your students to look for examples in their textbook of those patterns.

4. Have students discuss why different material was organized by the author in particular text patterns.

5. Encourage your students to use signal words to recognize text structure patterns.

As students learn to recognize the academic language words that signal common text structures and the patterns used to organize concepts, they will be able to make better connections with the core content contained in the text. Various text structures use different academic language words to signal their presence. Academic language provides important signals for informing the reader of the type of organizational or syntactical structure used by the author. Textbooks that are constructed using such text structures are easier to read, understand, and remember.

TEXT STRATEGY 4: CAUSE-EFFECT TEXT

Cause-effect text structures, also known as problem-solution text, describe the causal relationship between two things, where one thing creates a subsequent result in another thing. Authors use this type of text structure to show relationships, organize correlated factors, or show changes in results. For example, if we run into a fire hydrant with our car, the impact would be the "cause," and the damage to our car would be the "effect." Trying to determine why things happen as they do or striving to create a solution is a basic human drive. Cause-effect and problem-solution text structures are often used to teach concepts in social studies and science textbooks. Students who are struggling readers, special needs learners, or second language learners will need explicit instruction in text structures to support comprehension. Even though some textbooks may be effectively designed and clearly written for their student audience, the teacher is a vital part of making the various text structures explicit to students. Understanding the cause-effect or problem-solution text structure is important, as our students learn the basic ways the world works.

What Cause-Effect Text Looks Like

Cause-effect text structure uses the process of identifying a problem or concern and then provides potential solutions to address the issue in an orderly way.

Types of Cause-Effect Text Structure

- *Clearly stated cause-effect relationships.* The author explicitly uses the terms *cause* and *effect* in the text to show relationships.
- *Unstated cause-effect or problem-solution relationships*. Students should be taught how to "read between the lines."
- *Causal chains*. In this kind of text structure, one effect goes on to cause the next effect, which may then cause another effect, and so on.

Cause-effect text can be easy to comprehend if simple relationships are analyzed. This type of text can also represent complex relationships. In advanced placement or college texts, often a cause creates multiple effects or an effect is created from multiple causes. Causal analysis, which analyzes reasons (causes, problems, or factors) and subsequent results (effects, solutions, disadvantages, benefits, impact, or consequences), is an important benefit of cause-effect or problem-solution texts. Developing students' abilities to engage in causal analysis can contribute to students' higher-order thinking skills and ultimately to their writing skills. Examples of academic language signal words that show a series of cause-effect events include *therefore, if . . . then, for one thing, eventually,* and *for another.* Examples of academic language signal words that show causes or problems include *because, since, for, one cause is,* and *another reason.* Examples of academic language signal words that show effects or solutions include *as a result, consequently, so,* and *thus.*

How Cause-Effect Text Works

Instructional strategies that have been found effective in teaching the cause-effect and problem-solution text structure include

1. Discussing with students the importance of text signal words that help identify key text structures.

2. Explicitly instruct students in signal words that show cause-effect or problem-solution relationships: *because, so, so that, if . . . then, consequently, thus, since, for, for this reason, as a result of, therefore, due to, this is how, nevertheless,* and *accordingly.*

3. Explicitly instruct students on how to connect the different kinds of cause and effect relationships between key concepts.

The following example, from an eighth-grade science textbook, highlights some key signal words that students should learn to recognize.

Whenever there is a net force acting on an object, the forces are unbalanced. Unbalanced forces will cause the velocity of an object to change. The object can speed up, slow down, or change direction. Unbalanced forces acting on an object result in a net force and cause a change in the object's velocity. (Frank, 2001, p. 376)

This paragraph uses the academic language terms *result, change,* and *cause* to clearly state that this text is organized to show a cause and effect relationship that exists between force and velocity. The textbook does a good job of making the relationships clear to middle school students. The introduction provides the following text structures and suggestions for teachers and students:

- Preview Text Structure
- Preview Visuals
- Sequence
- Compare and Contrast
- Analyze Cause and Effect
- Identify Main Ideas
- Identify Supporting Evidence
- Create Outlines

As teachers scaffold instruction by helping students recognize signal words and casual analysis relationships, the resulting effect will be that students will improve their abilities to identify new information and comprehend concepts.

TEXT STRATEGY 5: COMPARE/CONTRAST TEXT

Compare/contrast is one of the most basic patterns of recognizing and retaining information. In the earliest grades, ideas and information are often organized in a compare/contrast fashion. Comparing or contrasting requires children to think about the very specific attributes or characteristics of the thing that they're observing and studying. Comparing promotes academic language development, concept development, and higher-level thinking development. In addition, comparing or contrasting gives students a cognitive strategy to help them mentally organize and retain the information they are learning. Comparing is a strategy that supports learning in all subject areas whenever two or more similar items in a category can be compared.

What Compare/Contrast Text Looks Like

Simply stated, compare/contrast text provides a process of identifying how things are alike and different. *Comparison* refers to how two things are similar or alike; *contrast* refers to how they are different or opposite. Categories may include different kinds of mammals, historical events, languages, chemical compounds, geographic regions, characters, math functions, bones, and so on.

Patterns of Compare/Contrast Text

- The *whole pattern* of compare/contrast texts discusses the first issue in its entirety, and then the second issue is discussed and comparisons or contrasts are noted.
- The *part-to-part pattern* of compare/contrast texts looks at a common element that is shared, and similarities or differences are noted. Then another common element is compared or contrasted.
- The *combination pattern* of compare/contrast texts looks at two or more main ideas and compares or contrasts them, going back and forth and addressing supporting details.

Graphic Organizers like T-charts or Venn diagrams can help to organize the comparisons or contrasts provided in text. Consider Table 5.4, which shows a T-chart of comparisons and contrasts.

Table 5.4   Comparison/Contrast T-Chart

Orange	Apple
Comparisons	
Fruit	Fruit
Round	Almost round
Grows on tree	Grows on tree
Size of baseball	Size of baseball
Contrasts	
Peel skin	Eat skin
Orange	Red, green, yellow
Sectioned and juicy inside	Mealy inside
Harvest in winter	Harvest in fall

The compare/contrast texts that students encounter are often a variation of different compare/contrast structures.

How Compare/Contrast Works

A number of instructional strategies help children develop an understanding of what comparison is and use that concept to support learning, reading, and writing. Because an advanced compare/contrast text structure can require the evaluation and analysis of a significant amount of information, some students will need support. Instructional Strategies that are effective in helping students comprehend the compare/contrast text structure include

1. Explicitly instruct students in the academic language that signals the compare/contrast structures. Examples of comparison signal words include *similar, like, still, likewise, in the same ways, in comparison, at the same time,* and *in the same manner.* Examples of contrast signal words include *however, on the other hand, but, yet, nevertheless, conversely, rather, on the contrary, nonetheless,* and *in contrast.*

2. Explicitly instruct students in several kinds of compare/contrast text structures.

3. Explicitly instruct students in the use of Venn diagrams and other means for organizing comparative information that can support both reading and writing.
   Have them write at a young age too

Depending on the concepts being considered, compare/contrast text structures can be very basic or very complex in their organization. This text pattern provides an efficient method for organizing even advanced concepts and data.

TEXT STRATEGY 6: DESCRIPTION TEXT

With informational text, the key is to grasp the main idea or central concept of the message and build from that point. All text structures have a main idea and then organize the supporting details in different ways. Description text relates the information in a rich, detailed format. Whether it is called the thesis, the topic statement, or the main idea, it is important that students can sift through information and determine the main issue being presented by the author. It is also important for the student to connect the supporting details and examples to the main idea, while still enjoying the descriptive language. The sooner students can determine the main idea of the text and differentiate the main ideas from the supporting details, the better students will understand expository text. Struggling readers often confuse supporting details with main ideas and visa versa. As a result, they are often unable to effectively organize their minds around the content contained in the text or gain insights from the context of the topic. Students who are able to determine the main ideas and then make connections to important supporting details are able to unpack the author's intent and generate their own meaning from the text.

What Description Text Looks Like

Descriptive text explains information typically in a hierarchical fashion, where the most important information is described first, and then additional supporting concepts and details are provided. Description texts:

- Describe the main idea
- Describe supporting concepts

- Describe key processes
- Describe important details

Consider the following vignette from a fifth-grade teacher as she shares one of her experiences with text structure in the classroom:

> I was excited to share my enthusiasm and the rich language contained in the text with my students. I recognized that some of my students would be able to engage easily with the text, others would look for encouragement, and others would need explicit scaffolded instruction. I front-loaded the lesson by explicitly outlining four words off of my academic language list contained in the text (*transform*, *probability*, *furthermore*, and *maximize*). I asked students to chorally pronounce the words. I gave them working definitions for each word. I provided examples from the text, and I invited my students to share how they could use these words in a variety of contexts.
>
> After my students read the text, I asked students to pair up and share with each other the main ideas they identified from the text. I then asked two smaller groups to combine and, as a larger group of four to share the supporting details for the main ideas with one another. My students used academic language, identified text patterns, and summarized the major themes with supporting details. The results paid off as all of my students significantly increased their comprehension of the material, and they increased their confidence in their learning abilities.

As we help our students become aware of the organization of information and the words that add description, we will see the text come more alive for our students.

How Description Text Works

A number of instructional strategies help children develop an understanding of descriptive text and support learning, reading, and writing. Instructional strategies that are effective in helping students comprehend the description text structure include the following.

1. Help students identify the main idea or central theme.

2. Make sure students identify supporting concepts and the examples that support the concepts.

3. Support students as they identify key processes and the important steps in these processes.

4. Ask students to identify important details that will help them remember the information.

5. Give students repeated opportunities to distinguish the main idea from supporting concepts and distinguish key processes from important details.

TEXT STRATEGY 7: SEQUENCING TEXT

Teach how do something to do it good [handwritten annotation]

Time-Order or sequencing refers to putting actions or events in a chronological order. Chronological ordering is common when outlining historical events. Another example of sequencing is the ordering of steps to carry out a process or procedure like those listed in manuals, instructions, and recipes. Explaining the life cycle also uses a time-ordered format. Of all the text structures, time-order or chronological sequencing is typically the easiest for students to understand. As children, students were introduced to stories that were formatted in a time-ordered series of events like beginning, middle, and end. Students also order many of the experiences in their lives in a chronological sequence. Being able to recognize the order of events helps with reading comprehension for children's stories, literature, and historical events. Quickly identifying the sequence of time-ordered events also helps students break large tasks into smaller, more manageable tasks, and students are able to comprehend the information more easily.

What Sequencing Looks Like

Sequencing information can occur for a variety of purposes in order to align things in time, space, or order of importance.

- Chronological or time-order
- Priority of importance
- Spatial order
- Formulas
- Order of process or step-by-step procedures

In addition to recognizing the sequencing of information, our students should also practice putting new information into a proper sequence (e.g., timeline, recipe, or appropriate steps).

How Sequencing Works

Instructional Strategies that have been found effective in helping students understand the sequencing commonly used in time-order text structure include the following.

1. Explicitly instruct students in the academic language that signals sequencing, that is, words such as *first, next, then, initially, before, after, when, finally, preceding, afterwards, as soon as, during, immediately, initially, later, meanwhile, next, not long after, now, preceding, second, soon, then, third, today, until, when,* and *following.*

2. Explicitly instruct students in the use of graphic organizers, particularly timelines.

3. Explicitly instruct students in their ability to ask probing questions to discern the sequencing pattern, for example:
   - What is being described?
   - Why is the sequence important?
   - What are major steps in this sequence?

Recognizing the time-order of events supports reading comprehension for stories or historical events, and it also provides a foundation for breaking large tasks into manageable pieces that must go together in a proper order.

TEXT STRATEGY 8: CONNECTING TEXT

An important part of explicit instruction is asking students to make personal connections to a text. Questions regarding text structure can follow a pattern of connecting text to self, text to text, and text to world. Connecting text to self improves relevance, while connecting text to text improves rigor, and connecting text to world improves relationships. Students can ask a variety of questions that will connect the text to their own understanding and experience (Rosenblatt, 1991). When students make a variety of connections with text, their learning improves (Keene & Zimmerman, 2007).

What Connecting Text Looks Like

Developing connections with text creates the skills for students to become life-long learners who can use books to help direct their learning.

Connecting With Text

- Connecting *text to self* helps students explore thinking
- Connecting *text to text* helps students extend understanding
- Connecting *text to world* helps students expand meaning

As students become comfortable connecting with text, they will further explore, extend, and expand their thinking and understanding.

How Connecting Text Works

This strategy uses questions to get students to interact and connect with the text in ways that increase their knowledge.

Connecting Text to Self

1. Ask students to make a connection from information in the text to something they already know.
   - What do you already know that is related to the information in the text?
   - Does this remind you of anything in your life?
   - How does this information relate to your life?

2. Ask students to make a connection from someone in the text to someone they already know.
   - Whom do you know who is similar to this character in the story?
   - How is this similar to your own life?

3. Ask students if something in the text reminds them of any of their previous experiences.
   - Has something like this ever happened to you?
   - What have you experienced that is similar or different?
   - What were your feelings when you read this?

Connecting Text to Text

1. Ask students to make connections from the information in the text to other texts they have read.
   - What other information have we studied that connects to the concepts in this text?
   - How is this text similar to other things you've read?

- How is this different from other books you've read?
- Have you read about something like this before?

2. Ask students to make connections from characters in the story to other characters in other books.
   - What other characters from stories you have read faced similar experiences or reacted in similar ways?
   - What does this remind you of in another book you've read?

3. Ask students to make connections between the ways the author organized the patterns of text to other similar text patterns.
   - What is the pattern of the text?
   - What other texts do you know follow a similar pattern?

Connecting Text to World

1. Ask students to make connections between the information in the text and some real-world applications of the information.
   - What does this remind you of in the real world?
   - How is this text similar to things that happen in the real world?

2. Ask students to make connections between the experiences in the text and situations they may face in the future.
   - What can you learn from this character that will help you succeed in your future?
   - How is this different from things that happen in the real world?

3. Ask students to make connections between the way the text is constructed by the author and how they structure their own writing.
   - How has the author constructed the text?
   - What can you learn about good writing from the way this author structured the text?

SUMMARY

As students develop their understanding of various text structures and the academic language that signals these structures, their ability to comprehend concepts contained in the text will improve. Students, like Kim, enjoy reading narrative stories, yet will the same enthusiasm be expressed as text becomes increasingly complex and more information based? Knowing academic language and key signal words, which identify text structures, will help our students analyze informative text and succeed with the literacy demands of school. Knowledge, even in its simplest forms, has thousands and even millions of connections between classifications, subjects, categories, descriptions, and qualities. Understanding the actions, relationships, and transitions between these various connections is crucial as our students learn and broaden their knowledge. As our students learn how to make sense of the organization of text structure, then their ability to comprehend the concepts contained in the text will increase. As we help our students better recognize the signal words that reveal informative text structure, they will be able to make meaning from the text and retain content knowledge. By identifying text structure, asking questions of the text, and organizing key concepts in the text, students will have the best opportunity to keep up with a rigorous pace of learning and even accelerate their ability to bridge the gaps in their language, literacy, and achievement.

PERSONAL REFLECTIONS

1. Currently, how do my students strategically approach classroom text?

2. Which of my students know the various types of text structures for the assigned readings in my class, and how will I help those who struggle?

3. How many of my students use signal words to identify the expository text structures to help them organize their learning?

Academic Listening Strategies 6

Words are the voice of the heart.

—Confucius

Kathlan's Story

Kathlan loved listening to her teacher tell stories. She learned about places she had never heard of before. She could picture characters and scenes, and she imagined that she was an actual part of the experience. Her mind would just seem to open up, and it felt free to wander and wonder as she sat quietly in class. Every day, Mrs. Tribblehorn would also read out loud a science article about new discoveries, technologies, or interesting animals in the world. Kathlan just knew some day she would discover or possibly invent something that would make a real difference. Her quest to accomplish this feat made every math and science lesson seem worthwhile. And of course, social studies was important too, because she would travel and learn as she crossed the globe. Learning new words also became part of her desire. To be ready to listen and to read whatever she could, she knew, would help in her pursuit for learning more knowledge. She knew, at the very least, that she would become a teacher someday and take time to travel to exciting destinations and read about other wonderful far-off places to her students.

ACADEMIC LISTENING AND ACADEMIC LANGUAGE

Before we ever produce language, we listen to the language patterns of others. Children in Australia listen to their parents and others around them, and then they eventually produce similar language to what they have heard. In another part of the world, children in China listen to very different sounding words, and then they produce words that symbolize similar concepts, yet sound very different from those children in Australia. Similarly, students learn the academic language registers of school when they direct their attention to the important skills of academic listening. Sarosy and Sherak, (2006) acknowledge that academic listening encourages students to pay attention to the language of lectures and listen for topics so they become familiar with the expressions that signal how teachers proceed with instruction. Academic listening is the crucial first step to understanding academic language and a vital part of developing academic literacy. Carrasquillo and Rodriguez (2002) point out that "Listening is the central process in daily language use. . . . However, educators often neglect teaching listening skills to students." (p. 84). This is particularly the case in content-area classrooms. Kasper, Babbitt, and Williams (2000) add, "There are few that address listening and speaking skills. This is unfortunate because academic success requires competence not only in reading and writing, but also in listening and speaking" (p. xi). Developing academic listening helps students become active participants in their classroom learning. Of all the literacy modes, listening may be the most underappreciated, underrated, and overlooked.

DEVELOPING EFFECTIVE LISTENING COMPREHENSION

Students who develop academic listening also improve their abilities in academic comprehension. The ability to listen and identify academic words, to understand the meanings of these words, and to recognize the language structures surrounding them is a powerful predictor of a student's successful comprehension (Muter, Hulme, Snowling, & Stevenson, 2004). Comprehension of spoken and written language is highly reliant upon a student's knowledge of individual word recognition and word meaning (McGregor, 2004). Developing academic language is intricately tied to success in both listening and reading comprehension. Each of the modalities of communicating—reading and writing, listening and speaking—contribute to successful comprehension (Gernsbacher, Varner, & Faust, 1990). Thus, students who lack academic language face significant challenges developing comprehension as they listen to spoken discourse.

LISTENING STRATEGY 1: ACTIVE ACADEMIC LISTENING

Listening actively to content-area instruction begins each student's journey to becoming an active participant in academic discourse. Good listeners monitor their understanding, so it is important for our students to generate questions in their mind and consider what they already know and what they still need to learn. Active listeners distinguish the main ideas and connect them to supporting ideas and details to create meaning. Students need to hear the words as spoken correctly by the teacher so that meaning can be properly constructed. Students should be able to infer the meaning of words from the context of teachers' comments and their intonation. Listening is a process of actively directing attention to the words and conceptual understanding of classroom content. Look at the average percentage of time spent by students in core classroom literacy modes (Rubin, 1994):

Literacy Time

- Listening—50% of class time
- Speaking—25% of class time
- Reading—15% of class time
- Writing—10% of class time

[handwritten marginalia: "IDK if I agree w/ this 2"]

Listening is the number one activity that students are expected to master within the classroom.

What Active Academic Listening Looks Like

Academic listening is an interactive, two-way process between the speaker and the students. Good academic listeners continually anticipate and predict potential connections, while consistently assessing their understanding. The following list (adapted from Powers, 1985 and Richards, 1983) emphasizes several important academic listening skills. Students need to be able to

- Identify purpose and scope
- Identify topics and their developments
- Identify major themes or ideas
- Recognize key academic language
- Identify relationships among major ideas
- Recognize the role of discourse markers that signal structure (signal words)
- Identify supporting ideas and examples
- Retain information through note taking
- Infer relationships between information
- Retrieve information from notes
- Identify the spoken mode of lectures
- Recognize the function of intonation, pace, pitch, volume, key, and so on
- Use highlighting, handouts, and PowerPoint to support their learning

[handwritten note: Active Listener Chart in classroom!]

An important part of academic listening is for students to hear and hold complex and compound sentences in their mind while they make connections and understand related ideas.

How Active Academic Listening Works

This strategy helps students develop an arsenal of active listening strategies to keep themselves engaged and learning effectively. Effective teachers ask various types of questions (adapted from Dunkel, 1993) to demonstrate listening and aid understanding.

1. Ask listeners to sort out why they are listening and what they want or need to know.

2. Invite listeners to predict some of the information to be included in a lecture, and have them assess how much of the incoming information will be new and how much will be familiar.

3. Refer students back to their initial reason for listening; listeners should determine how much of the message is going to be relevant to the purpose of the task or the initial reason for first listening.

4. Ask Listeners to check their understanding of the message in a variety of ways. (E.g., questions, gestures, and responses.)

5. Finally, students should share their answers in a classroom discussion to compare what they were thinking and processing as they listened to the academic instruction or lecture.

LISTENING STRATEGY 2: UNDERSTANDING LISTENING PURPOSES

Improving listening skills develops our students' ability to think critically, respond intelligently, and collaborate effectively. Yet, many of our students are often unaware of their listening habits and the important role academic listening plays in understanding. Listening comprehension actually precedes and prepares students for reading comprehension (Gough & Tunmer, 1986). They should be introduced to listening skills so they can gain greater awareness of their personal listening strengths and weaknesses. Our students will be able to more actively attend to the speaker when they know their primary purposes for listening.

What Listening Purposes Looks Like

A variety of objectives establish the primary purpose for listening. Teachers should encourage students to ask, "Why am I listening?" or "What is my purpose?" Students should be able to identify the following purposes.

- Are you listening **to understand and follow instructions?** Students should listen to the specific directions and instructions provided. They should keep an open mind as they execute the expectations.
- Are you listening **to receive information and remember?** Students should listen first for the main ideas and how the communication is organized. They can then connect primary points to secondary details.
- Are you listening **to seek enjoyment and be entertained?** Students should listen for those sensory elements that enhance imagery and the five senses. Humor and comical language can enhance the mood and make the experience fun.
- Are you listening **to empathize and give support?** Students should listen closely to connect with others' feelings and respond appropriately.
- Are you listening **to examine and evaluate?** Students should ask themselves about the speaker's qualifications and if the message is legitimate. They should be alert to errors, sweeping generalizations, appeals to emotion, and charged words that attempt to distract from the facts.

Often, these listening purposes are combined in a message, and students who listen effectively are better prepared to master the purposes of school.

How Listening Purposes Works

This strategy encourages students to be conscious of how they focus their attention. Students often have little awareness of their literacy skills as listeners. You can give your students the following inventory, so that they can recognize and reflect on important skills and focus on the purposes of academic listening.

Listening Inventory

Students should be encouraged to articulate their level of listening by asking themselves the following questions. Do I

1. Interpret a speaker's message, purpose, and perspective?

2. Identify new vocabulary and listen for context clues?

3. Distinguish factual statements from opinion?

4. Recognize key ideas and concepts from supporting information?

5. Identify emotions through cadence, pitch, pauses, and speed?

6. Recognize the speaker's mood?

7. Listen critically to formal presentations?

8. Listen attentively to others while acknowledging and building upon their ideas?

9. Listen to others' viewpoints respectfully, making eye contact, verbal responses, and appropriate gestures to show I'm paying attention (head nods, etc.)?

10. Anticipate where the speaker is going in the conversation and confirm by listening attentively?

11. Filter out distractions, external noises, voices, traffic, and so on?

12. Filter out distractions such as internal disinterest, anxiety, and prejudice?

13. Listen while critically analyzing and evaluating experiences, ideas, issues, and information?

14. Reflect on how talk varies in different situations?

15. Listen for the social, historical, and cultural context of various perspectives?

16. Listen for the purpose of connecting information to prior knowledge, making conceptual connections, discovering relationship patterns, recognizing key themes, and remembering main ideas and supporting details?

When our students become aware of the many important listening skills, they can then direct their attention and listening more effectively to the content of messages being delivered in their classrooms.

LISTENING STRATEGY 3: ACADEMIC LANGUAGE AWARENESS

When our students listen in class, they may be quite unaware of the academic language being spoken that is essential to academic success. The number one obstacle in the way of successful listening comprehension occurs when students are unaware or lack understanding of key academic terms (Kelly, 1991). Developing students' conscious awareness of academic language will help them listen more attentively and understand more clearly. Properly identifying concepts and naming them accurately is an important step for improving academic listening and developing "elaborative" comprehension (Rounds, 1987). Word awareness supports active listening and metacognitive awareness. As students listen attentively and then reflect on what they are hearing, they process at deeper levels of understanding. Braunger and Lewis (2005) note that students who are

> learning academic content require more intense and intentional scaffolding to bridge from their experience to the content of the text, develop appropriate schemata, build understandings of context, and internalize academic language. For these students it is important that teachers not simplify but rather amplify and enrich classroom language to support the development of academic concepts. (p. 61)

What Academic Language Awareness Looks Like

It is exciting to see students engage in learning the specific-content language of various disciplines. Teachers who increase their students' awareness of the words that convey important concepts open up a world of understanding. Beck, McKeown, and Kucan (2002) assert that, "The teacher who is alert to opportunities for using sophisticated, interesting, and precise language is probably the most important element in a word-rich environment" (p. 159). Understanding academic language will help students process explicit instruction and teacher dialogue by recognizing signal words. Students typically have varying levels of academic language awareness and word consciousness. Gaining academic language understanding takes a consistent effort by both teachers and students. According to Francis et al. (2006), students require, in multiple contexts, up to14 encounters with a word and its definition before they understand it thoroughly. Teachers should evaluate students' level of word knowledge in order to measure their level of comprehension.

Four Levels of Understanding Word Knowledge

1. I never saw it before.

2. I've heard of it, but I don't know what it means.

3. I recognize it in context—it has something to do with . . .

4. I know it! (adapted from Dale & O'Rourke, 1986)

As our students develop their listening skills they will improve their overall understanding.

How Academic Language Awareness Works

Language awareness helps students consciously appreciate the ways in which words organize our ideas and help us to understand others.

1. Invite students when listening to classroom instruction to key in on the academic language words.

2. Have students write down academic words and categorize them into action, concept, and transition language.
   - *Actions.* The first step students should take is to listen carefully to the action words that the message is predicated upon.
   - *Concepts.* Next, they should listen for key concept words and focus on the ideas that convey the content.
   - *Transitions.* Last, students should recognize transition words that connect the ideas.

3. Invite students to rate their level of understanding of words according to the four levels of understanding word knowledge.

4. Students should then be placed in small groups and see if their peers can provide a working definition, examples, nonexamples, antonyms, synonyms, or a picture of words that received a rating of three or lower.

5. If groups are still unable to answer questions at least at level 3 (*I recognize it in context*), then you should provide explicit instruction (see Strategy 5 in this chapter) to help students learn these words.

6. Remember, students need twelve to fourteen exposures to develop understanding at level four (*I know it!*).

As our students increase their awareness of key academic language in repeated and overlapping content-area conversations, then they will truly "know" the terms that will expand their literacy.

LISTENING STRATEGY 4: PROVIDING QUALITY OBJECTIVES

A key component to helping our students listen is to be clear in our communication with them. Students need explicitly stated objectives to provide a focus for their learning and listening. Objectives reveal the purposes, the direction, and the intended results that guide content-area learning. Objectives should make clear the actions you want students to execute internally and demonstrate externally, as well as the standards for the performance of those actions. Objectives should also include the content that will be covered. Quality objectives refer to learner behavior rather than teacher behavior. Writing powerful learning objectives requires a shift from what the teacher will do to what students are expected to do at the end of the lesson.

What Quality Objectives Look Like

Listening is a purposeful activity, and students need objectives or points upon which they can focus their attention. Instructional objectives provided in content-area classrooms should be

S hort-term
M easurable
A ction Oriented
R eviewable
T argeted

SMART objectives specify why students should listen, outline what they are expected to be able to do, and define how they should perform.

How Quality Objectives Work

The SMART strategy works effectively when objectives include all five key components.

Five Principles of SMART Objectives

1. Know your audience and identify age-appropriate expectations that can be achieved in the *short-term*.

2. Identify content knowledge that will be *measured* (e.g., math operations, science principles).

3. Make clear the internal *actions* that students should execute (for example: synthesize, interpret, reflect).

4. *Review* the external actions of production that demonstrate learning (for example: write, answer, create, list).

5. Outline the *targeted* performance standard expected (for example: answer fifteen questions, write two paragraphs, list four examples).

Additionally, you should write the daily objective on the board and ask a student to read it out loud; help clarify the measurable expectations of the objective; provide your students with a quality objective that addresses the zone of proximal development for their age group (i.e., grade level standards); and check to make sure at the end of the lesson that the students demonstrated their accomplishment of the objective.

Consider the following sample objectives that are closely aligned with many state standards. Notice the action, transition, and concept words that dominate the message of most formal objectives.

1. *Demonstrate* knowledge of grade-appropriate words in classroom text; *in addition, identify* sentence and word *context* clues to *explain* important *relationships* between the words.

2. *Solve* simple equations like adding and subtracting fractions *while writing* the answer in simplest form.

3. *Identify* the *structures* and *processes* by which flowering plants generate pollen, ovules, seeds, and fruit.

4. *Explain* how scientific inventions and technological advancements in the late 1800s led to *social, cultural,* and *economic* changes *while also* setting the stage for the industrial revolution.

When our students can quickly identify and easily comprehend the key language outlined in classroom objectives, they will be prepared to successfully achieve the objectives.

LISTENING STRATEGY 5: ACADEMIC LANGUAGE SCHEMATA

Viewing information graphically is an important part of developing schemata or the patterns that structure knowledge. Students often need instructional scaffolding to help them build a schema and explicitly define important language terms. Scarcella (2003) points out that explicit instruction in language schemata directly affects the resulting comprehension for students. Building a schema starts with learning a specific term that can connect to a variety of ideas, characteristics, and relationships. Without academic language, it is difficult for students to effectively build their schemata or knowledge structures. Jacobs (2006) demonstrates this with the following math example:

> [A student] needs practice listening to you and knowing how to ask a clarifying question. He may be using conversational language rather than academic language, referring to the denominator as the "bottom thing" and the numerator as the "top thing"; he may refer to mathematical operations using imprecise language, muddling mathematical thinking in his own mind. (p. 4)

The ultimate objective of explicit instruction is the development of academic schemata and student learning.

What Academic Language Schemata Look Like

Providing explicit instruction ensures that skills, processes, and concepts are explicitly understood by each learner. Oftentimes the term *explicit instruction* is synonymous with *direct instruction*. Direct instruction typically emphasizes the teacher and the process of teaching, while explicit instruction places the emphasis on the learner and the level of her or his engagement and understanding. Explicit instruction evaluates instruction from the actions of the learner, rather than just the actions of the teacher. Explicit instruction should move systematically from initial teacher input and extensive modeling to group interaction and finally to individual student responsibility for learning.

Preparing Learners to Listen to Explicit Instruction

1. Introduce academic language and specific-content language.

2. Build background information.

3. Connect instruction to prior knowledge.

4. Motivate student interest and explain relevance.

How Academic Language Schemata Work *Graphic Organizer*

This strategy is at the heart of learning academic language. Students should follow this seven-step process and fill out the academic language graphic organizer on a daily basis. The following steps will improve students' knowledge of academic language and provide a consistent format for learning new words.

Explicitly Learning Academic Language

1. **Write the academic word.** Students will benefit from spelling the word. They can also write other words in the word family (e.g., *complete, completion, completing,* and *incompletion*).

2. **List synonyms.** Writing down similar words will help describe and connect the word to the student's prior knowledge.

3. **List examples.** Writing down examples will provide a real-world context for the word.

4. **Provide a working definition.** Students who generate their own definition remember the word much better.

5. **Draw a picture.** The act of drawing will provide a symbol for remembering.

6. **List antonyms.** Identifying contrasting words will provide greater clarification for students.

7. **List nonexamples.** Writing negative examples will provide a greater context for the word. (This may be challenging to complete for abstract actions.)

The following graph (6.1) pictorially represents this strategy for learning academic schemata.

Let's look at Graphs 6.2 and 6.3, which populate the academic language graphic organizer using examples from science and mathematics.

The seven-step academic language graphic organizer can be filled out by students and hole-punched so that the words and the supporting schema card can be collected on a ring and easily be referenced by students. As students add graphic organizer cards to their ring each week, they will be impressed with how many words they have added to their academic vocabulary.

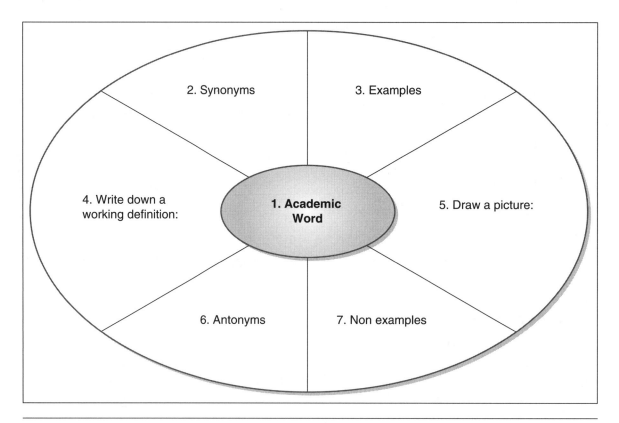

Graph 6.1 Academic Language Graphic Organizer

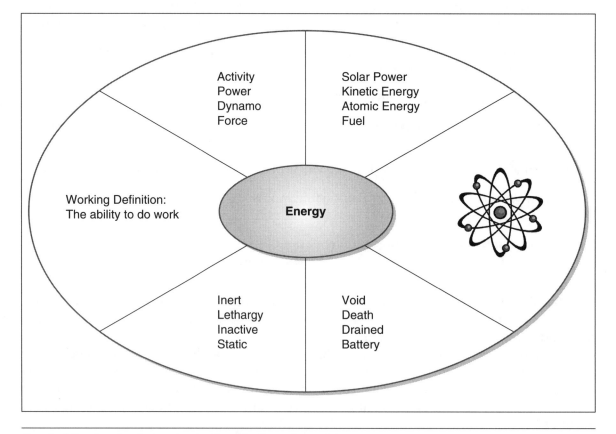

Graph 6.2 Academic Language Graphic Organizer—Science

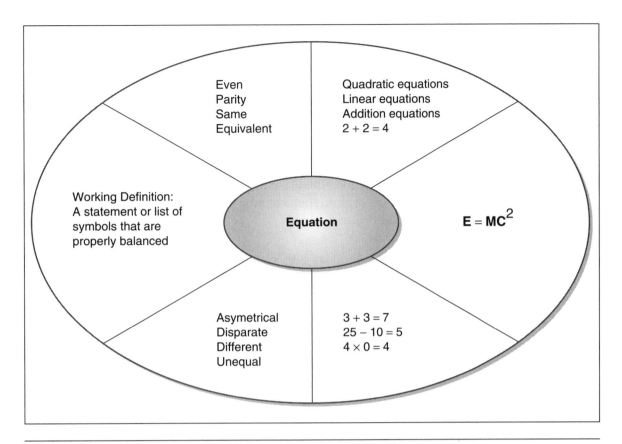

Graph 6.3   Academic Language Graphic Organizer—Mathematics

LISTENING STRATEGY 6: CONTENT-AREA THINK-ALOUDS

Think-alouds can be modeled for students in all of the content-areas. Each discipline has important processes for developing knowledge and creating solutions. Teachers can demonstrate these processes and share out loud whatever they are thinking, doing, or feeling as they conduct a task. Fisher and Frey (2008) emphasize that

> The key to an effective think-aloud is that the teacher is using the first person to describe how he or she makes decisions, implement skills, activates problem-solving protocols, and evaluates whether success has been achieved. Importantly, this is a chance for students to witness how an expert merges declarative, procedural, conditional, and reflective knowledge in a fluent fashion. (p. 31)

Think-alouds are particularly helpful in math and science, which present a wide variety of operations and procedures.

What Content-Area Think-Alouds Look Like

You want to explain the internal processes going through your mind and model this for your students as you go through an important thinking or learning process in your content-area (hypothesis, report, following instructions, mixing chemicals, analyzing social behavior, conducting an experiment, etc.). Content-area think-alouds allow us to model important steps of the learning process (adapted from Harvey & Goudvis, 2007). In them, we may

- Share aspects of the inner conversation
- Show how to check predictions and understanding
- Share how we activate and connect background knowledge
- Pretend to struggle to understand something
- Share our questions
- Share our inferences
- Verbalize confusing points and demonstrate fix-up strategies
- Share how we sort and sift information to determine important ideas
- Pause to make conclusions and summarize

How Content-Area Think-Alouds Work

Teachers should consider the following six steps when presenting a think-aloud to their classes:

1. Begin by considering specific processes (e.g., creating a hypothesis, gathering information, writing a report, or reading challenging text) for students to think through, analyze, and actively process in their minds.

2. Choose one strategy and think-aloud process and consider the what, why, and when of each strategy. With older students, you can think-aloud several cognitive strategies at one time (e.g., making predictions, activating prior knowledge, and summarizing information).

3. Make sure you outline the purpose of the thinking process.

4. Go through the process and stop every so often, even in mid sentence, and share how an effective thinker would engage in the strategy. Use the think-aloud process to help students identify the following strategies:
   - Connecting
   - Predicting
   - Questioning
   - Monitoring
   - Prioritizing
   - Visualizing

5. Make specific statements regarding your thinking as you go through the process:
   - So far, I've learned . . .
   - This made me think of . . .
   - That didn't make sense.
   - I think _____ will happen next.
   - I reread that part because . . .
   - I was confused by . . .
   - I think the most important part was . . .
   - That is interesting because . . .
   - I wonder why . . .
   - I just thought of . . .

6. After you have modeled a think-aloud with your students, you should model a variety of think-alouds with the different types of academic strategies used in class.

Notice that think-alouds expect students to engage in similar cognitive strategies to those they should use while reading. Through think-alouds, you will be able to develop your students' abilities to think critically and engage effectively in the learning processes of your academic discipline.

LISTENING STRATEGY 7: ACADEMIC NOTE TAKING

In academic note taking, students listen and evaluate which information has more significance, and they take these main ideas or themes and build supporting information and evidence around it. The first listening skill is skimming, where the listener quickly seeks to obtain the gist of the speaker's purposes. The second listening skill is scanning, where the listener strives to obtain specific information regarding relevant points made by the speaker. Studies on academic listening (DeCarrico & Nattinger, 1988; Chaudron & Richards, 1986) note that students who recognize explicit signals in the organization of instruction develop better comprehension. An important habit to develop when taking notes is to listen and record key words, clues, hints, patterns, and other connections. Listening processes exist in real time. Therefore, teachers should be aware of the rate at which they speak, so their students have time to properly listen. People speak at an average rate of 150 words per minute in casual conversations. Teachers speaking to their students should typically slow down to about 100 words per minute when introducing new information.

Rate of Speaking

- Fast speaking speed is 220 words per minute
- Average casual speaking speed is 150 words per minute
- Slow speaking or formal speaking speed is 100 words per minute

Anderson-Hsieh and Koehler (1988) observed that slower speech rates by teachers, when introducing new information and material, helped all student retention. Yet, the slower speaking speed also created some potential concerns for some students. Consider, how fast do students listen? Or, to put the question in a better way, what is the average number of words per minute that students normally process as they listen? Nichols (1948) discovered that students listen and think at four times the average rate of conversation. If all their thoughts were measurable in words per minute, the answer seems to be that an audience of any size will average 400 to 500 words per minute as they listen. The challenge becomes the differential between the speaker communicating at 100 words per minute and the average student's ability to think and process at 400 or 500 words per minute. Most students are unaware of the differences in the rate at which they can hear distinct sounds (100–220 words per minute) and the rate at which their mind can think and operate (400–500 words per minute). Students should be encouraged to use the "rate gap" to take notes, decipher inferences, and make multiple connections between ideas. Unless they are actively engaged, listeners can easily be lured into a false sense of security and start wandering mentally rather than fully engaging in the listening tasks at hand. Academic note taking can help students engage in the instruction and create a written document for future review.

What Academic Note Taking Looks Like

When students listen to the teacher, the action of taking notes helps students focus their attention and concentrate on the subject at hand. The kinesthetic activity of writing helps many learners process information more efficiently, make sense of the incoming subject matter, sift through information, and identify and record the most vital information that will help trigger long-term memory of the information for future use. Rost (1990) emphasizes the following important actions when organizing classroom notes:

- Identifying key words or phrases (academic language)
- Ordering or grouping related information, underlining main points, and drawing arrows for connections (academic organizing)
- Using highlighting, parenthesizing, bulleting, and numbering (active emphasis)

Effective note taking should be accurate, clear, and concise. The notes should reflect the organization of the content, so that it may more easily be remembered. Students should recognize the main purpose and points of the speaker. They should identify key language or new terminology.

How Academic Note Taking Works

Students should write important information whenever the teacher

1. Gives a specific example
2. Asks if everyone understands
3. Makes a direct reference to a book
4. Points or gestures to information
5. Writes information on the board or overhead
6. Repeats information
7. Slows down and transitions
8. Makes a connection between categories of information

Note-taking strategies should explain and illustrate the important concepts. Students should be shown how to take notes in outline form, make predictions, follow instruction, assess their understanding, and summarize key information (Pauk, 1997).

Note-Taking Method

- **Record.** Write down the important relevant information in the note-taking column on the right and place main ideas with supporting details and information under it.
- **Reduce.** Synthesize the key language and main ideas in the cue column. Connect key concepts and clarify relationships. This reinforces continuity and enhances memory. Summarize in a sentence or two the main ideas, write down questions.
- **Recall.** Cover the main column and see if you can remember the information from your cues and summarize important concepts and language in your own words. This helps to transfer the key information to your long-term memory. If recitation occurs within 24 hours then up to 80% retention can occur.
- **Reflect.** Develop opinions and make meaningful associations from the concepts, relationships. Reflect by labeling, classifying, outlining, categorizing, and summarizing key ideas. Make additional connections to other material learned. Classifying and creating categories helps to remember information for future use and tests. Write down questions that you are still seeking answers to.
- **Review.** Every week take ten minutes to go back over notes and see if you have remembered the important information and connected it together.

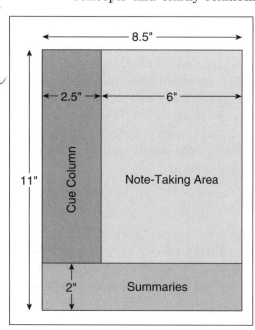

Figure 6.1 Page Setup for Note Taking

Figure 6.1 shows a diagram for an orderly note-taking page setup.

The note-taking process should recognize important networks and links between ideas, because the relationships, transitions, and connections between key concepts develop deeper understanding.

SUMMARY

As your students learn to listen to you and practice good habits of academic listening, their learning will increase. Students like Kathlan tend to listen effectively, because they are focused on achieving, yet all students can improve their listening comprehension and academic literacy. Listening is the first literacy skill that students develop. Academic listening, like academic language, is often taken for granted, and not explicitly taught, because students are immersed in listening to language all day long. The question becomes, "Are students sinking or swimming as they listen to the academic language shared with them in the classroom?" Explicit, daily instruction in academic language is at the heart of academic listening. As students learn additional academic language, they will be better prepared to read, learn, and write. The academic language schema graphic allows students to develop their understanding of new academic terms in depth. Creating a notebook for academic language schemata can serve as a resource for future learning. Academic listening can be difficult to observe, unless students are asked to display their listening through completing objectives, communicating comprehension, and taking effective notes. Academic listening is a talent that all students can develop, yet improving this skill takes consistent practice and attention. Students should focus on the academic content of instruction by listening for the actions, relationships, transitions, and key concepts conveyed in the classroom. Students can benefit from listening to academic discussions as they take notes, ask clarifying questions, and construct meaning.

PERSONAL REFLECTIONS

1. How aware are your students of their level of attention, and in which areas of academic listening can they make improvements?

2. What is your daily routine for explicitly introducing new academic language and vocabulary to your students?

3. In what ways do your students listen effectively and take notes to provide a record of their learning?

7 Academic Speaking Strategies

One of the hardest things in life is having words in your heart that you can't utter.

—James Earl Jones, actor

Guillermo's Story

Guillermo grew up in the Imperial Valley of California just across the border from Mexicali. He was born a U.S. citizen, yet he spoke his parents' native Spanish in the home, and he struggled through his first four years of school. Guillermo could speak English well enough around town, yet he rarely spoke at school while his parents worked long hours in the field and sacrificed for his future. The less he said, it seemed, the simpler things went at school. At lunchtime, Guillermo would speak Spanglish with his friends, yet he never made any attempts to speak academic language in the classroom. The academic tasks and concepts of school intimidated him, and he sat by idly watching the teacher along with many of his fellow students. Like many second language learners who are immersed in different languages at home versus the one spoken at school, avoiding academic talk had become the way of existing in the classroom. Each day at school seemed to follow the same dull pattern. He could speak English in his neighborhood, which was more than his parents were able to do, yet his academic progress seemed to stall. Because he spoke so infrequently, the gaps in his learning grew larger as he spent time in school. His learning seemed to have hit a low plateau. The first year or so of school seemed okay, yet his disengagement was starting to catch up. Ms. Jordan, Guillermo's fifth-grade teacher, wondered how it would all turn out, while the dizzying boredom pushed Guillermo one more step toward the door and toward a shaky future.

ACADEMIC SPEAKING AND ACADEMIC LANGUAGE

Students learn best when they are engaged and actively participating in the learning process. Discussion expects students to listen to information and then comment or respond. When students engage in discussions, they need very direct language or dialogue tasks as well as specific content or concept tasks. In schools, the amount of high-level talk about text, challenging assignments, student-centered instruction, and high levels of student engagement prove to be a significant predictor of student achievement on a variety of measures (Taylor & Pearson, 2002). Students from poverty and those that lack the academic language of school often avoid participating in the academic conversations at school. Feldman and Kinsella (2005) note that it is often only the teacher who uses academic language, while students listen. Feldman and Kinsella go on to add, "We must structure daily classroom contexts so that all students are accountable for using newly introduced terminology in their speaking and writing" (p. 8). The prospect of engaging in these conversations seems risky and potentially embarrassing for many students. But instructional conversation in academic language, cognitive strategies, and peer-to-peer dialogue increases student learning, particularly for those who struggle in school (August & Shanahan, 2006).

Traditional Teacher Talk

Traditionally, teachers talk for a significant portion of the school day. They dominate the communication that happens in most classrooms. Often, teachers are more concerned with getting students to quit talking than engaging them in quality conversations. Students who lack confidence in academic language and literacy skills often avoid participating in class and try to limit situations where they are expected to contribute answers. Instructional interventions work best when students engage in structured discussions that build formal language registers and keep students on task (Kinsella, 2007). Researchers found that academic conversations comprise only a half a percent of the 1,500 classes they observed (Learning 24/7, 2005). When so little of the classroom dialogue is devoted to rich academic conversations, understanding stalls, and learning languishes.

Most classroom conversations are teacher-centered with the typical inquiry-response-evaluation (IRE) format, rather than a student-centered approach with a focus on sharing ideas and stimulating discussions. The IRE model begins with a question, and the student is expected to give the "right" answer. The IRE model of teacher interaction has extremely limited instructional benefits. IRE interaction ends with teachers evaluating student responses, rather than students reflecting and extending their thinking (Cazden, 1988).

Traditional IRE Model *Bad Sometimes*

Initiating question by teacher to the whole class

Response by one student (often the first to raise their hand)

Evaluation by teacher of accuracy of response

In the IRE model, only one student responds at a time and the responses are usually "right" or "wrong." The kind of learning that lends itself to IRE patterns of instruction is limited to lower-level thinking and emphasizes recall of information. Questions aimed at producing accurate recall or simple identification do not tend to promote in-depth thinking. It is good to ask students questions, yet when the teacher is looking for a very specific answer and only one person responds at a time, it can quickly become a case of "guess what the teacher wants us to say." After giving explicit instruction, teachers should engage students more and talk less. Students, particularly teenagers, like to know what their classmates think on matters and will listen attentively so long as the discussion is appropriately structured.

ACADEMIC LANGUAGE AND CLASSROOM DISCOURSE

Each content area has a discourse language, and it is important to become familiar with the patterns and themes that currently make up the collective thinking of the particular content area. Content-area discussions should focus on topics within the discipline and the academic reading within the textbooks. But, students often quietly take themselves out of the academic discourse of content-area classrooms, and eventually they take themselves out of school, as they drop out and become academic casualties. We should combat this by teaching not only academic listening but also academic speaking. Learning core content includes a process for laying a foundation in academic language that allows students to access core content. This academic foundation begins with the literacy skills of listening and should soon support the transition into academic speaking. Wilkinson and Reninger (2005) highlight the following benefits of content-area discourse.

Benefits of Classroom Discourse

- Students who are of average ability and below benefit most from class discussion approaches for learning about content-area topics.
- Students can help each other learn through collaborative communication.
- Encouraging small-group talk about a content task promotes both academic learning and social learning.
- The more opportunities students receive to engage their peers in dialogue, the greater improvement in the quality of student talk.

The academic discourse spoken in various content areas serves as a precursor to the professional discourse that is vital to building a quality career. Leadership counts extensively on communication skills, and communicating effectively or "talking the talk" at work is part of becoming a valued leader. Paired conversations and structured small-group talk amongst peers can go a long way. The following three group structures provide important opportunities for students to develop their academic speaking skills.

1. Whole-Group Discussions

2. Small-Group Structured Talk

3. Paired-Academic Conversations

If teachers only ask questions and call on the first to shoot a hand up, they are failing to engage all of their students in academic discourse. Adger and Wolfram, (2007) emphasize, "All children need linguistically rich classrooms in all subject areas to develop expertise in literacy and in academic talk, the genre of language used in teaching and learning, and in business and professional settings" (p. 127). The smaller the groups, the more involvement, yet for the teacher it can be more challenging to monitor communication. The larger the group means less individual involvement, yet the teacher is able to monitor and direct the discussion more easily. Pair-shares are an excellent initial activity to get students to speak to a peer and see how their ideas sound. Underconfident students can hear their own comments out loud to see if they like what they have said, and they often receive positive reinforcement from their peers to share their good ideas.

SPEAKING STRATEGY 1: CONTENT-AREA CONVERSATIONS

Engaging instruction is orchestrated like a structured conversation. Instructional conversations are very different from casual conversations or the IRE that dominates many classrooms. Instructional conversations are about internalizing structures of content topics. Engaging in academic talk prepares students to access textbook language. Brisk, (2005) notes that "Teacher-student interaction is practiced through instructional conversation. This instructional strategy develops academic language and content as well as thinking skills. In these engaging conversations between the teacher and a small group of students, learners have the opportunity to practice the language and negotiate their thoughts with the teacher and peers" (p. 179). Compare the spoken conversation statistics in Table 7.1 with those for printed texts in Table 7.2, noting rare words (both tables adapted from Cunningham & Stanovich, 1998).

Table 7.1 Rare Words in Spoken Conversations

Spoken Conversation	Rare Words per 1,000
Expert witness testimony	28.4
TV cartoon shows	30.8
TV prime-time children's shows	20.2
College graduate speaking to spouse and friends	17.3
TV prime-time adult shows	22.7
TV Mr. Rogers and Sesame Street	2.0

Table 7.2 Rare Words in Written Texts

Printed Texts	Rare Words per 1,000
Abstract of scientific articles	128.0
Newspapers	68.3
Popular magazines	65.7
Adult books	52.7
Comic books	53.5
Children's books	30.9
Preschool books	16.3

What Content-Area Conversations Look Like

Students need to know that academic conversations can be much more challenging than casual conversations. Table 7.3 shows some of the significant differences between academic conversations and casual conversations.

Table 7.3 Casual and Academic Conversations

Casual Conversations	Content-Area Conversations
Here and now context	Decontextualized
Personal interest	Academic issues
Concrete subjects	Abstract ideas
Casual language	Academic language
Social relationships	Concept relationships

Show the diff — multilingual Rhymes!

Academic talk is organized more like printed text, and it emphasizes the use of academic language. Teachers need to structure literacy activities in their classroom where students feel they can succeed. While doing a meta-analysis of seventy-five research studies, it was found that collaborative discussions that focused on a critical analysis of text or asking specific higher-order questions of ideas contained in text had a positive and consistent effect on successful reading comprehension results (Murphy & Edwards, 2005).

How Academic Conversations Work

This strategy works as it helps students extend, expand, and increase the quality of their thinking and classroom conversations. The following ten principles for leading classroom dialogue support quality academic conversations (adapted from Saunders & Goldenberg, 2007).

1. The teacher selects a theme or idea to serve as a starting point for focusing the discussion.

2. The teacher either "hooks into" or provides students with pertinent background information and relevant schemata.

3. When necessary, the teacher provides direct teaching of a skill or concept.

4. The teacher elicits more extended contributions from students by inviting them to expand, by posing questions, and by restating.

5. The teacher promotes students' use of text, pictures, and reasoning to support an argument or position.

6. Much of the discussion centers on questions and answers for which there might be more than one correct answer.

7. The teacher is responsive to students' statements and the opportunities those statements provide.

8. The discussion is characterized by multiple, interactive, connected turns; succeeding utterances build on and extend previous ones.

9. The teacher creates a "zone of proximal development," where a challenging atmosphere is balanced by a positive, affective climate.

10. The teacher encourages general participation among students.

Also, matching low-level learners with friendly students who are in the mid-range can be better for students than partnering them with students with highest level of academic language.

SPEAKING STRATEGY 2: STRUCTURED DISCUSSIONS

Students like hearing the ideas of their peers. Yet the question becomes how does one keep students in pairs and small groups on task? Students can easily digress. The key is providing them with a clear direction and holding them accountable for their conversations. Francis and colleagues (2006) simply declare, "Ideally, teachers would plan for structured opportunities to practice language, model effective questioning and conversational practices, and gradually turn over the responsibility to students for peer-led discussions and conversations" (p. 28).

What Structured Discussions Look Like

The following discourse practices benefit all students, as they increase many of the communication skills they are taught at home. For the many students who lack these skills, consistent practice will improve the quality of classroom dialogue. Students should practice these classroom speaking skills daily.

Structured Discourse Skills

1. Express Opinion
2. Paraphrasing
3. Asking for clarification
4. Soliciting a response
5. Acknowledging others' ideas
6. Reporting a partner's ideas
7. Reporting a group's ideas
8. Offering a suggestion
9. Agreeing
10. Holding the floor

The communication skills used in effective discourse may be common for some students, yet most students in school will need plenty of practice to become proficient in effective discourse. Langer (2001) observes that in the higher performing schools, at least 96% of the teachers helped students engage in the thoughtful dialogue we call shared cognition. Teachers expected their students to not merely work together, but to sharpen their understandings with, against, and from each other. (p. 31–32)

How Structured Discussions Work

This strategy works when teachers make sure that students understand effective discourse practices and can participate appropriately in classroom discussions. Students can be given the following sentence frames to help them engage in paired, small-group, or large-group discussions.

1. Select three speaking skills from the following list for your students to practice as you give them a content-area issue to discuss.

2. Each student should provide follow-up responses to show that they are actively engaged in the discussion.

3. Ask your students to use the sentence frames or sentence starters to help them participate in the discussion and provide feedback to their peers.

This strategy uses sentence frames to provide a framework or scaffold for students to support effective classroom discourse. The sentence frames get student dialogue started in the right direction and keep the students engaged in effective discourse (adapted from Kinsella, 2007).

Paraphrasing

- So you are saying that . . .
- In other words, you think . . .
- What I hear you saying is . . .

Asking for Clarification

- What do you mean?
- Will you explain that again?
- I have a question about that.

Soliciting a Response

- What do you think?
- We haven't heard from you yet.
- Do you agree?
- What answer did you get?

sounds like Socratic Method

Acknowledging Others' Ideas

- My idea is similar or related to _____'s idea . . .
- I agree with _____ that . . .
- My idea builds upon _____'s idea . . .

Reporting a Partner's Idea

- _____ indicated that . . .
- _____ pointed out to me that . . .
- _____ emphasized that . . .
- _____ concluded that . . .

Reporting a Group's Idea

- We decided/agreed that . . .
- We concluded that . . .
- Our group sees it differently . . .
- We had a different approach . . .

Disagreeing

- I don't agree with you because . . .
- I got a different answer than you.
- I see it another way.

Offering a Suggestion

- Maybe we could . . .
- What if we . . .
- Here's something we might try . . .

Agreeing

- That's an interesting idea.
- I hadn't thought of that.
- I see what you mean.

Holding the Floor

- As I was saying . . .
- If I could finish my thought . . .
- What I was trying to say was . . .

Teachers need to plan and organize classroom discussions, whether they are large- or small-group discussions, in ways that structure the thinking and conversations to engage students in using academic language. The following eight steps are an excellent way to structure discussion pairs.

Structured Discussion Pairs

1. Place students in pairs. Each pair should have a short paragraph of text that they read. Explain that they will read and have to make one significant statement to summarize their ideas about the reading.

2. Model taking turns, providing interpretive comments, and receiving feedback.

3. The first student makes a significant comment about the reading.

4. Next, the second student may respond (agreement, disagreement, clarification, offering a suggestion, etc.).

5. Then the students switch, and the second student shares his or her significant comment.

6. Now, the first student has the opportunity to respond.

7. Students alternate reading several short paragraphs relating to their significant summarizing statements, and they then listen to one response.

8. To add accountability to the conversations, you may want to ask students to write out their summarizing statements before reading them out loud. This way, you can track the quality of their ideas to make sure students are getting the gist of the reading.

When teachers structure classroom discussions with sentence frames and academic language, students have a clear direction to take their thinking and learning. Although these discussions are initially directed by the teacher, the teacher acts primarily as a facilitator to the dialogue. As classes become proficient at responding to one speaking function, you can add additional speaking functions to accomplish in a single discussion. You may ask students to both clarify and acknowledge the thoughts of others. With practice, students will soon become proficient, and they will be able to model academic conversation for each other while the teacher can positively acknowledge good ideas, nice presentations, and overall improvement. It will take several weeks for students to begin to feel comfortable with all of the speaking function.

SPEAKING STRATEGY 3: ACADEMIC TALK

Academic talk is structured talk that extends and expands student understanding. Wolfram, Adger, and Christian (1999) note that "Meanings are usually made more fully explicit through words in academic talk. Language may also have different functions in academic interaction than in family or community interaction" (p. 127). Again, using sentence frames is an excellent way to teach academic talk. They provide students with a comfortable framework to structure their classroom conversations. Sentence frames give students a common starting point, yet the students direct the end results of the discussion. Sentence frames or sentence starters can be used to introduce students to new academic language and connect content-area concepts.

What Academic Talk Looks Like

Academic talk is content-area talk that is scaffolded by the classroom teacher to support academic processes and get positive academic results. In academic talk, students practice

- **Tapping prior knowledge**
- **Predicting**
- **Picturing**
- **Internal questioning**
- **Asking questions of others**
- **Making connections**
- **Generalizing**
- **Forming interpretations**
- **Clarifying issues**
- **Relating the conversation back to their learning**
- **Summarizing**
- **Reflecting on their learning**

How Academic Talk Works

Classroom discussions between peers in small groups or pairs provide students with important opportunities to develop their ability to learn. When students produce language and communicate with their peers, the academic talk helps students become more consciously aware of the important cognitive strategies that develop academic literacy. Like the speaking habits that we want students to develop. Students also need to develop cognitive thinking habits as they engage in Academic Talk.

Tapping Prior Knowledge

- I already know that . . .
- This reminds me of . . .
- This relates to . . .

Predicting

- I guess/predict/imagine that . . .
- Based on _____, I infer that . . .
- I hypothesize that . . .

Picturing

- I can picture . . .
- I can see . . .
- I imagine . . .

Internal Questioning

- A question I have is . . .
- I wonder about . . .
- Could this mean . . .

Asking Questions of Others

- I wonder why . . .
- What if . . .
- How come . . .
- How is it possible that . . .

Making Connections

- This is like . . .
- This reminds me of . . .
- This is related to· . . .

Generalizing

- So the big idea is . . .
- The general impact is . . .

Forming Interpretations

- What this means to me is . . .
- I think this represents . . .
- The idea I'm getting is . . .
- One question that this text answers is . . .
- One question that this text raises is . . .

Clarifying Issues

- I'm confused about . . .
- I'm not sure about . . .
- I didn't expect . . .

Relating the Conversation Back to Learning

- This is relevant because . . .
- This concept relates to . . .
- As I learned about _____, I also thought about . . .
- The concept I found most provocative is . . .
- This proposal could be more effective if . . .

Summarizing

- So the main point is . . .
- The conclusion I am drawing is that . . .

Reflecting on Learning

- The most important concept I learned today was . . .
- My favorite comment from a classmate was . . .
- The most challenging part of our project was . . .

Academic Talk Activity: Jigsaw Discussions

Select four passages from a text the class is currently studying.

1. Students are placed in groups of four.
2. Each student is provided with and carefully reads one of the passages.
3. Students highlight the main idea or gist of the passage.
4. Students identify information supporting the main idea.
5. Students make statements and ask questions using the academic talk sentence frames (making connections, generalizing, clarifying issues, etc.) as guides.
6. Students use academic language and each take turns sharing their sentence frame responses about their reading passages with their peers.
7. Students summarize together and create a shared meaning that they generate from their conversation about the four passages.

SPEAKING STRATEGY 4: ACTION CLOZE STRATEGIES

Students should work in pairs to negotiate the answers and determine which actions most effectively fit each sentence. Barrier activities are classroom activities that are specifically designed by the teacher to make sure students will speak to each other so that instructional objectives can be accomplished (Gibbons, 2002). Engaging students in barrier activities is an extremely effective way to ensure that students must speak and listen to each other in order to complete a task. One student should be given the answers and the other students should be given the sentences with action word blanks.

What Action Cloze Strategies Look Like

Cloze strategies are generally designed to help teachers determine students' level of prior knowledge and word recognition in a content area. The action cloze strategy is a great tool for quickly determining the reading level for each student. This strategy requires students to use their background knowledge and textual context clues to figure out which word accurately fits in each blank. Select an engaging content-area passage with approximately 250–300 words; texts can contain shorter passages for younger learners and longer passages for older learners.

How Action Cloze Strategies Work

Partner Action Cloze Exercise

1. Type or copy and paste text on a page, making it double spaced.
2. Delete the action words, and create blanks in each sentence. Create a list of the words deleted from the passage.
3. Before filling in any blanks, students should read the entire passage to get the context of the passage and of each sentence.
4. Have students place the word they believe fits into each blank by analyzing the context of each sentence, using the exact word they believe the author chose.
5. Each blank should contain only one word, and there is only one right answer for each blank.

6. Misspelled words are counted correct, yet close synonyms are incorrect.
   - Under 40% correct means the text passage is too difficult.
   - Between 40–60% correct means the text passage is just right.
   - Above 60% correct means the text passage is too easy.

Students who struggle with a text that is too difficult need additional help developing their knowledge of academic language action words (relinquish, consider, etc.). Teachers should continue to work on explicit instruction strategies (see Chapter 6, Strategy 5) to support this type of academic language.

Following is an example of an action cloze exercise. Please fill in the blanks with the appropriate action words, or verbs that the author used. Use the following action words (some words may be used more than once).

> relate, blow, draw, measure, talk, keep, compile, make, use, wear, observe, record, know, read, changes, use, tell, collect, keep, make, watch, use, match, measure, invite, measure, look

Elementary Science Tasks

A. _____ simple weather instruments and observations to _____ and chart weather data in a periodic journal throughout the year. Look for patterns.

B. _____ or listen to stories about the weather and _____ the stories to observations.

C. _____ what you _____ about weather patterns and how the weather _____ through the year and during different seasons to _____ an illustrated booklet relating changes in temperature and rainfall to seasonal changes.

D. _____ bubbles or _____ a pinwheel to _____ the wind's direction and strength.

E. _____ a weather booklet with pictures or drawings of different clouds, precipitation, and weather events.

F. _____ for rainbows. _____ when and where you saw them on a class list. _____ what was happening in the weather when you saw it. _____ a story about rainbows to find out more about them.

G. _____ the stories you write for the booklet to _____ about how weather affects what people wear and what games they play.

H. _____ pictures of what to wear during different kinds of weather or _____ pictures of the weather with articles of clothing. (For example, _____ a coat, hat, and gloves when it is very cold.)

I. Scientists _____ all forms of precipitation in a rain gauge. They _____ sleet and snow by letting it melt and then measuring it in a rain gauge. _____ a weather person (meteorologist) to _____ to the class about measuring precipitation.

J. _____ a container or rain gauge in the school yard and _____ the precipitation. _____ a record to _____ for wettest months and driest months.

Action cloze exercises can also be done in groups, small or large. Below is an example of a small-group action cloze exercise.

1. Select a passage from a text the class is currently reading.
2. Delete the action words, creating blank spaces in the text, and use these deleted words to make the word list students will draw from to fill in the blanks.
3. Place your students in groups of three.
4. Next, ask your students to read through the passage and insert what they believe is the word the author of the text chose to best fit the context of each sentence. The group should discuss and negotiate their ideas and then choose the best word.
5. Afterwards students can share with the whole class the thinking behind their decisions as they selected the words to insert in the blanks.

A cloze activity can pique students' interest as they focus on the academic language, and it will challenge them to link concepts to the context of their reading. Cloze activities stretch students' understanding and cause them to consider the multitude of actions that govern our operations. In the process of figuring out the actions or predicates of each sentence, the students also learn about classroom content.

SPEAKING STRATEGY 5: TRANSITION SEQUENCING

The purpose of transition strategies, like all of the academic language strategies, is to teach content while also teaching students the language patterns that help organize information according to relationships like problem-solution, compare/contrast, cause-effect, time-order. One exercise for teaching transition sequencing is to have students prepare a reciprocal teaching lesson that, for instance, compares/contrasts storybook characters, for their peers.

Use the following transition sequencing words and phrases to show comparison: *like, still, similarly, in the same way, likewise,* and *at the same time.*

Use the following transition sequencing words and phrases to show contrast: *but, however, yet, nevertheless, conversely, in contrast,* and *on the other hand.*

What Transition Sequencing Looks Like

- It is important that students be able to determine the order of time, space, importance, and so on.
- Academic language signal words can help determine the proper sequencing of events.
- Students can also use the context of each sentence to determine the proper order.

Make 'n' Break Strategy

For the following exercise, ask students to read each sentence. Then cut them out and lace each sentence in the order the author originally intended. Instruct students to use the flow of ideas, context clues, and the transition words in the sentences (*as, most important, consequently,* and *eventually*) to reconstruct the original order. (The following sentences are from Franklin Institute, n.d.)

1. As he matured, Ben used his diplomacy skills to serve his fellow countrymen.

2. Most important, Ben stands alone as the only person to have signed all four of the documents that helped to create the United States: the Declaration of Independence (1776), the Treaty of Alliance, Amity, and Commerce with France (1778), the Treaty of Peace between England, France, and the United States (1782), and the Constitution (1787).

3. Benjamin Franklin stands tall among a small group of men we call our Founding Fathers.

4. Consequently, no other individual was more involved in the birth of our nation.

5. He actually helped to write parts of the Declaration of Independence and the Constitution.

6. His role in the American Revolution was not played out on the battlefields like George Washington, but rather in the halls and staterooms of governments.

7. Eventually, his clear vision of the way things should be, and his skill in both writing and negotiating, helped him to shape the future of the United States of America.

The original sentence order was 3, 1, 6, 7, 2, 5, and 4.

SPEAKING STRATEGY 6: LIST-GROUP-LABEL CONCEPTS

List-group-label is an inductive learning approach (Taba, 1967). Through inductive learning, students consider a set of data and then organize and group the data in patterns. The exciting thing about this strategy is that students often will come up with similar yet different ways of organizing the data. Students will recognize that there are multiple ways of grouping information and recognizing patterns in their learning. Because there is no exact way to group the data, as long as each student follows the strategy's parameters, they will be learning. Students can share in small groups or with the class their method for thinking about the material, and students will see a variety of ways that information can be organized. This will help students develop their academic language and categorization skills. Students also are able to get practice in organizing content-area concepts. This process helps your students learn and remember the words and concepts, because each student sifts through and organizes the material in their own personal way. This strategy helps students recognize similarities and differences, and it will help students engage with content-area concepts and work with the language and concepts associated with the content area. The first time this strategy is employed, you may want to go through and do a think-aloud to share the decisions that went into your categories and labels.

What Concept List-Group-Labels Look Like

Inductive learning moves through five essential phases. They describe how your students should experience the learning.

1. Examine data

2. Group and label data

3. Interpret information

4. Synthesize the information

5. Evaluate the lesson

How Concept List-Group-Labeling Works

The following exercise can be adapted to any content area. Simply use concepts, equations, or formulas, locations, types of terrain, or types of governments, dates, and so on.

1. Provide students with a list of words that are related in various ways, and place the students in groups of three or four, so they can discuss the list.

2. Students brainstorm ideas to determine how the words are related and group them.

3. Students discuss and negotiate with their partners to decide which items will go into each category.

4. Tell students to group data with common attributes—group at least three and no more than nine items in a category.

5. Students should give descriptive labels to the categories they decide upon.

6. Students share with the rest of the group their category labels and their thinking as they grouped and labeled the items on the list.

7. Students discuss different ways they organized words and concepts.

8. Reconvene students in a whole-class discussion, and ask students to share how they grouped categories and made decisions.

For an alternative approach, the teacher can place a concept on the board and students can brainstorm as many words that they believe fit into that category to establish the list. Older students can organize entire sentences. Younger students enjoy cutting out sentences or words and placing them in categories. Following is a list of academic language words.

List-Group-Label

• Realize	• Furthermore	• Significantly	• Example
• Imply	• Nevertheless	• Additionally	• Purpose
• Include	• Consequently	• Strategy	• Principle
• Identify	• Finally	• Function	
• Exemplify	• Similarly	• Approach	
• Moreover	• Eventually	• Scaffold	

SUMMARY

Students need opportunities to discuss classroom content and express their developing ideas. Students value dialoguing with their peers, so that they can hear others ideas and articulate their own. Many content-area classrooms give students few opportunities to really engage and discuss important topics related to the discipline. Students benefit significantly from discussing content topics with their peers. Hearing others ideas and speaking about the issues being learned in class helps shape students' thinking. Speaking causes students to consider and reflect on the development of their ideas. As students are expected to use academic language in their responses, they gain a greater appreciation for the positive, yet challenging, environment that can be created. Academic speaking is purposeful and structured. Sentence frames provide a precise format for students to follow that helps them keep on task and direct their focus to discussing the academic content.

PERSONAL REFLECTIONS

1. How often do your students engage in structured academic talk?

2. What academic language do your students speak?

3. How successful are your students in using each of the various speaking functions?

Academic Writing Strategies **8**

The skill of writing is to create a context in which other people can think.

—Edwin Schlossberg, designer

Jerome's Story

Jerome stared down at his science report sitting on his desk. The report, with the big fat D on it, seemed to stare back at him. Emotions quietly began to build as he tried to swallow the feelings swirling around inside. While his mind raced through a maze of thoughts and reflections, he told himself, "This doesn't hurt—it doesn't matter." School seemed like a waste of time anyways, just a place for pointing out his weaknesses. He had even turned this paper in on time. He threw down enough words to fill a page or two. He knew it was a jumble of words and ideas that probably made little sense, yet he really liked this topic. He usually just blew off writing assignments and accepted the consequences. He thought, "It's not my fault that I don't really know how to write." He noticed others blankly glancing at their papers. He said to himself, "High school is too hard." Jerome felt one big step closer to dropping out. He wondered why he even came to school. It was just a big waste of time. Jerome looked over at his teacher and wondered how Mr. Williams had even sparked the hope that he could write. Mr. Williams had proclaimed that this was the year that they would learn how to write like scientists. Even though he felt many miles away from that goal, Jerome wondered, "Is this the year I am going to learn how to write, or is this the year I am going to drop out?"

ACADEMIC LANGUAGE AND ACADEMIC WRITING

Academic writing gives students the opportunity to synthesize the information they have learned while listening, reading, and speaking in class. In Jerome's case, he lacks the academic language and understanding of how to organize writing and capture his learning on paper. Academic writing is the hallmark of rigorous learning. Understanding academic language provides the basic tools for effective academic writing. Any type of writing can be challenging, since writers often receive no verbal feedback, no clarifying questions, and no written responses. And academic writing can be even more difficult than other forms, because the complexity of concepts and language is much greater than casual communication. Writing to the academic purposes of school requires specific strategies and practice that typically take time for students to develop. Francis et al. (2006) note:

> many facets of language are wrapped up in the notion of academic language, including vocabulary knowledge; understanding words of increasing complexity and length; and understanding complex sentence structures and discourse structure, including argumentation, narration, and exposition, and the corresponding syntax of the English language. (p. 15)

When we place higher academic demands on our students in the form of challenging writing assignments, literacy skills will increase for both higher- and lower-achieving students (Applebee, Langer, Nystrand, & Gamoran, 2003). As our students effectively combine the academic language of actions, transitions, and concepts, they will discover dramatic improvements in their writing. Consider the following dilemma that many teachers face.

Mr. Williams's Story

Mr. Williams felt reluctant to give the writing assignment, yet he knew over time it would make a big difference. He wondered what it would be like to teach in the wealthy suburbs where it seemed the kids liked to write. He hated giving out so many poor grades, yet everyone in the department committed to require more rigorous expectations from the students—and scientific writing is definitely rigorous. He knew his kids were struggling with understanding the textbook and in-class reading assignments. What was he thinking, hoping these kids could write scientifically? He was starting to regret the idea of asking his kids to write, even though he knew it was the right thing to do. He wondered how he could prepare his kids for the academic demands required to become an effective writer. If the kids were struggling with reading and speaking intelligently about important topics, why did he think they could write about them? He decided to start with a new approach: help the students practice a simple, one-sentence hypothesis and then work up to a thesis statement, next a paragraph with topic sentences, and finally short-answer essays. It seemed like it might take a while, yet in time, the students would learn the format of scientific writing and increase their understanding of the content at the same time.

CONTENT-AREA WRITING STRATEGIES

Effective writing generally follows the same format as that of blockbuster movies. Moviegoers enjoy films with colorful images, plenty of action, and developing relationships. Writers who can capture their audience's imagination and interest use descriptive language, action language, and language that shows relationships to effectively convey their ideas. A primary objective of academic writing is to develop a complete writing repertoire. The greater number of academic words a student knows, then the more precise and descriptive a writer can become. Our students need direction as they develop the skills and strategies that go into effective academic writing. Feldman and Kinsella (2005) clearly state, "All too often the teacher is the only individual in the classroom who uses actual academic language. If one of our instructional priorities is significantly narrowing the lexical divide, we must structure daily classroom contexts so that all students are accountable for using newly introduced terminology in their speaking and writing" (p. 8). Academic writing strategies ask students to focus on a specific skill and purpose for their essay, like persuade, compare, contrast, or analyze. Extensive research has shown that instructing our students in academic writing strategies will help them develop more effective thinking and learning skills. The following content-area writing strategies summarize the writing strategy research (adapted from Graham & Perin, 2007).

Academic Content-Area Writing Strategies

- Setting Specific Writing Goals or Tasks
- Writing for Content Learning
- Modeling Writing Strategies
- Using Descriptive Writing
- Sentence Combining
- Collaborative Writing
- Summarizing Text

As our students develop each of these specific content-area writing strategies, they will become effective academic writers. Let's look more closely at each of these valuable strategies for improving academic writing.

WRITING STRATEGY 1: SETTING SPECIFIC WRITING GOALS OR TASKS

Providing students with a clear purpose helps them successfully focus on the task. When writing, the first question students should ask is, "Why am I writing, or why has this been assigned?" or "What is my goal or purpose for writing?" Initially, the response may be to complete the assignment or get a good grade. Yet, the greater purpose for writing is to communicate a focused message to a particular audience. Outlining specific writing goals helps the writer approach the audience and helps the readers see the reasons for communicating. Writing with clear goals and purposes helps achieve functional literacy or the ability to use literacy to successfully function in society. Through functional literacy, our students can inform, persuade, explain, report, negotiate, evaluate, and problem solve. In a recent study by Fearn and Farnan (2005), they found that teachers who focused on the functions of language in the context of actual writing produced strong, positive effects on their students' writing.

What Writing Goals Look Like

Each writing assignment should be designed to achieve a specific purpose or goal. Much of the academic writing in school is to prepare students for the professional writing of the

---

Purposes for Writing

- Persuade
- Explain
- Negotiate
- Evaluate
- Analyze
- Problem Solve
- Compare/Contrast
- Investigate

workplace, where conveying information becomes a key priority. Most often, academic writing and professional writing looks to accomplish technical tasks.

Academic and professional writing may accomplish multiple purposes. For example, a business report may begin by informing the readers and then shift to persuading them to a particular point of view. Focusing on the purpose and goals of writing can help direct the writer's energy and efforts towards more effective results.

How Writing Purposes and Goals Work

This strategy works when students receive frequent opportunities to write and gain confidence in a variety of writing purposes. The goals or purposes of writing influence the writer in his or her selection of an appropriate topic, introduction, and thesis.

1. Share the purpose of the writing assignment with your students and explain how different purposes require different approaches to writing.

2. Discuss with students how the purpose of writing impacts the types of topics that will work effectively.

3. Help your students select an appropriate topic for the writing assignment.

4. Invite your students to write an attention grabber or opening sentence that supports the purpose of the writing assignment.

5. Connect the purpose of the writing assignment to a thesis. Each student should create a thesis broad enough to cover the scope of the topic and purpose.

6. Ask students to turn in a sheet that connects the purposes of the writing assignment to the topic, attention grabber, and thesis that they have created.

7. Finally, give feedback to all students, and specifically help those students who are finding it challenging to match the purpose to a topic, thesis, or attention grabber.

Students who clearly understand the purpose of their writing assignments and can select an appropriate topic, write an effective opening sentence, and design a focused thesis will be started in the right direction as they fulfill their writing assignments. Getting students off on the right foot accomplishes a lot in building their confidence as writers.

WRITING STRATEGY 2: WRITING FOR CONTENT LEARNING

Developing the ability to write with precision and clarity in formal settings expects students to use the academic language that articulates their understanding in a particular content area. Writing well is a talent that is developed through thoughtful instruction and plenty of practice. Yet, as Francis et al. (2006) note, "There is generally minimal focus on providing structured opportunities for the practice and production of academic language in the context of grade-level content as an important instructional goal in and of itself" (p. 28). Developing academic language literacy through content-area writing is valuable because improving the quality of student writing directly improves the quality of student thinking (Gopen & Swan, 1990). The purposes and decisions which go into writing in various disciplines can differ significantly. All of the content areas can explain important processes that reveal the key components of their particular subject matter. For example, even within science, different writing assignments may look very different. The purposes and processes for writing a hypothesis varies significantly from the purposes and processes that go into writing a nature journal. Content-area teachers need to explicitly model each various type of writing assignment for their students, and students should receive plenty of practice writing in a variety of content areas.

What Writing for Content Learning Looks Like

This strategy covers a variety of different formats or types of writing. As students learn to write different types of writing they will expand their writing repertoire. Consider the following types of content-area assignments.

Science Writing

- Creating a Hypothesis
- Conducting an Investigation
- Observations or Nature Journal
- A Scientific Report of Findings
- Compare/Contrast Essay of Natural Phenomenon

Mathematics Writing

- Constructing Data Tables and Analysis
- Creating Story Problems
- Explaining Mathematical Processes
- Method for Writing in Mathematical Notation
- Summary of Mathematical Concepts

Social Studies Writing

- Interviews of Historical Figures
- Compare/Contrast Social Issues
- Historical Research
- Responses to Reading Source Documents
- Biographies or Autobiographies of Historical Figures
- Arguing on Social Issues

Language Arts Writing   → Multimodal Narrative

- Writing Poetry
- Book Reports or Novel Summaries
- Expressive or Reflective Journals
- Analysis of Literature (Character, Plot, Theme, etc.)
- Persuasive Essay

How Writing for Content Learning Works

Because this strategy encompasses a wide variety of different writing assignments, it is important to think about the essential elements in each assignment. As teachers outline the key steps and processes in the different types of writing in our content areas, then our students will be better able to improve their writing abilities.

Modeling Science Example

1. Ask your students to select an object found in nature that they would like to study and then explain through writing (e.g., an elm tree, black ants, or honey bees).

2. Invite your students to observe the object firsthand, in nature, and record what they notice and see.

3. Your students should then synthesize their notes and identify at least three key characteristics of their object of study.

4. Take your students to the library and direct them to do research collected from at least five sources.

5. Ask students to connect their three firsthand observations with information provided in the research. These key observations can become three main topic sentences and the basis of a three-part thesis.

6. Your students should next write down at least two concrete details (facts or observations) for each of these key characteristics.

7. They should also make at least one comment (personal perspective) about why this characteristic is important. The concrete details and the commentary will serve as the main information in each paragraph.

8. Students should then be asked to write up their observations and research into a short essay to explain their object to others.

9. Note that because students are writing from their personal observations, their research connects to their understanding more easily, and their writing takes on more meaning.

10. Finally, students should prepare a three-minute speech from their writing assignment, and present their findings to the class.

When our students are taught the key steps in various types of writing, they will strengthen their ability to write effectively in multiple content areas.

WRITING STRATEGY 3: MODELING WRITE-ALOUDS

Modeling writing strategies for students can be accomplished through teacher write-alouds. Write-alouds are similar to read-alouds and think-alouds: In each, the teacher models and explains the processes behind these crucial literacy activities. Teachers should begin their modeling by making explicit the purposes behind content-area writing. For many students, teacher modeling provides crucial help in organizing the content contained in reading assignments, group discussions, and classroom note taking into cohesive writing. Teacher write-alouds should be used whenever students are given new writing assignments.

Another instructional approach we use often in our classrooms is writing-aloud in front of students. It is said that writing is the most complex of the elements of literacy (reading, writing, speaking, listening, and viewing) because it is built upon all of the others. In our view, writing aloud, which entails thinking aloud as one writes, is essential for improving writing among students (p. 35). When students observe teacher write-alouds, they are able to consider the important choices and decisions that go into constructing various content-area writing assignments. Thus, effectively modeling various content-area writing assignments is a crucial process for every content-area teacher. Students rarely receive modeling from adults on how to write effectively in different subject areas. Teachers in the various content-areas need to make explicit, through write-alouds, the practices and processes of effective writing within their specific discipline.

When students are able to observe their content-area teachers' write-alouds, they will be better prepared to effectively approach and construct content-area writing assignments. In modeling the scientific observation writing assignment above, for example, teachers want to model and explicitly state the thinking that goes into the decisions a scientist typically makes when recording observations and reflections in a journal. The modeling in teacher write-alouds demonstrates to students how writing works. Teacher write-alouds are helpful to students at all grade levels. As students get older, the modeling teachers share can become more abstract and complex. At all levels, teachers can solicit input from students for additional ideas on effectively writing the text. Lapp (2006) states, "The write-aloud lets the students in on what really happens as a writer constructs. Write-alouds are effective at any grade level" (p. 287). Content-area teachers have the ability to really impact student learning and help all of their students effectively understand and create writing within their discipline of study.

What Write-Alouds Look Like

Teacher write-alouds model the mental processes used to organize writing and reveal the physical processes used to construct writing assignments. The teacher can invite students to make suggestions as she or he creates the text. Students need teachers to model the organization and construction of various writing assignments and the purposes they serve as well as the different types of thinking and decisions that go into effectively completing various writing assignments.

Teacher write-alouds in the *early elementary grades* can model

- How to form and write the letters of the alphabet
- The proper placement of punctuation
- Capitalizing the first letter in new sentences
- Combining sentences using transition words like *and, but,* and *or*
- Indenting five spaces to begin a new paragraph
- Writing complete sentences

As students progress into the *upper elementary* and *middle school grades,* teachers can model

- The process of writing topic sentences that highlight main ideas
- The core content of the paragraph
- Writing effective paragraphs related to the specific discipline
- Writing effective summaries of classroom notes or texts
- Combining sentences using transition words like *since, for example, as,* and *because*
- Rewriting the main ideas in complete sentences
- Synthesizing notes into a piece of continuous writing

As students prepare for and enter the *high school grades,* content-area teachers can model

- The difference between main ideas and supporting ideas within the content area
- How to construct a central purpose statement or thesis
- The difference between concrete details (facts, data, quotes, etc.) and commentary (insights, opinions, interpretations, etc.)
- Combining sentences using transition words like *whenever, although, contrastingly,* and *notwithstanding*

- Identifying the relationships between the words and concepts through cause-effect, generalization, compare/contrast, and sequencing
- Changing the syntax or order of the text, rearranging words and sentences, changing verbs to nouns, adjectives to adverbs, and so on

Write-alouds, like read-alouds, succeed because they reveal metacognitive processes that occur internally. As teachers model their approach to thinking and writing within a specific discipline, then the students can hear the ideas and see the results of good writing.

How Write-Alouds Work

This strategy works because the teacher articulates metacognitive processes by thinking out loud and modeling writing processes in front of the students.

1. Start by sharing how you, as a writer, approach an assignment (for example, read the assignment and timeline, come up with a plan, etc.).

2. Next, discuss the purpose of the writing assignment and show how you connect your topic and thesis statement to the purpose.

3. Talk about how you approach the writing process and how it can differ for each writer's individual approach.

4. Let the students know that different writing assignments have different approaches. Be authentic, and talk as you write about your approach to various writing assignments (compare/contrast essay, observational report, etc.).

5. Ask the students questions, and check to make sure that they know all of the key components of the writing process.

6. Model each step of the process for them while talking about the decisions you are making as you proceed.

7. Tell students that writing in different content areas may follow different patterns or processes, and make sure you contrast the differences in various writing assignments (reports, essays, etc.).

8. Remember to encourage plenty of questions and keep a running dialogue with your students, continually talking about your approach and how you make writing decisions.

9. Ask students to follow the model you provide them, and invite them to share their feedback with you.

When students can see teachers working through the construction process of writing and they can hear the thinking and decision-making processes modeled by the teacher, they are better able to grab a pencil and effectively construct their own writing to meet the purposes of the assignment.

WRITING STRATEGY 4: USING DESCRIPTIVE WRITING

Similar to movies, a chief characteristic of good writing is the ability to use language to describe things in vivid, colorful detail. Descriptive language uses adjectives and adverbs, which describe in greater detail the concepts conveyed in the writing. Many content-area teachers know that writing helps students organize the information in their class, yet they can be reluctant at times to assign content-area writing because students are often unaware of how to effectively think and write within different disciplines. As content-area teachers explain important organizing and writing processes, students are able to shape their own understanding and thinking within the particular content-area. These adjectives and adverbs may be simple words like *fast, exuberantly, anxious,* or *surprisingly.* As students learn to use a wider variety of words, phrases, and clauses, they will be able to convey their ideas precisely and with plenty of description.

What Descriptive Writing Looks Like

— Teach grammar to help.
Thesarros
word of the Day

Descriptive language seeks to be precise and express the intricate characteristics of concepts. Descriptive writing occurs in three primary ways.

Descriptive Writing

1. Words (adjectives and adverbs)

2. Phrases (prepositional and verbal phrases)

3. Clauses (adjective and adverbial clauses)

Look over the following examples of descriptive words that describe the subject and the predicate or action.

Adjective Words

- *Fast* jet-planes
- The *anxious* applicant
- My *special* blanket
- The *jubilant* cheerleader

Adverb Words

- *Exuberantly* skipped
- *Surprisingly* sophisticated technology
- Ran *quickly*
- Ate *noisily*

Students who have a highly literate vocabulary and have been encouraged to use a good variety of words to describe subjects and actions will find that they are better able to express their ideas. Effective writers also understand how to use adjective and adverbial phrases to describe important events, and prepositional and verbal phrases to actively show relationships and provide further description. Students can become conversant with these phrases as they are provided practice.

Adjective Phrases

- The car with the hot-rod wheels
- The book on the shelf
- My friend from Timbuktu
- Plucked of all its feathers our goose for Christmas dinner

Adverb Phrases

- Jumped behind the curtain
- Sprinted between the tacklers
- Swam to the buoy
- Walked to get some gasoline

And finally, mature writers know how to use adjective and adverbial clauses to provide detailed description of their ideas. The easy thing about learning adjective clauses is that they all begin with relative pronouns. The five frequently used relative pronouns are *who, whose, whom, which,* and *that.* Adverbial clauses begin with subordinating conjunctions like *because, when, where, although, while,* and *since.* Adverbial clauses describe the actions associated with the verb.

Adjective Clauses

- A rooster, which crows at five o'clock in the morning, woke me up.
- The secret agent who fired the turbo jet got away from his assailants.
- Three employees that won the super lottery work at the same job.
- My butterfly, which emerged from a cocoon, flew away.

Adverbial Clauses

- The criminal ran when he spotted the police officer.
- Because the lithium atom added a proton, the chemical bond changed.
- The 18th Amendment outlawed liquor, although it was still easy to get.
- If you give me two dollars, I will get you some ice cream.

How Descriptive Writing Works

This strategy works as students realize that words, phrases, and clauses can provide detailed descriptions.

1. Invite students to choose a subject they would like to describe.

2. Ask students to suggest adjectives to describe this subject, and emphasize that improving description will improve writing.

3. Ask students to suggest phrases or clauses that could also describe the subject. If students struggle, you can share some of the words that begin adjective phrases (*for, with, on, from,* etc.) or clauses (*that, who, which, whose,* etc.).

4. Invite students to choose an action or predicate they would like to describe.

5. Ask students to suggest adverbs to describe the action.

6. Ask students to suggest phrases or clauses that could also describe the action or predicate of the sentence. If students struggle, you can share some of the words that begin adverbial phrases (*to, between, behind, over,* etc.) or clauses (*if, when, because, where,* etc.).

7. Ask students to practice writing the longest descriptive sentences they can while using as many descriptive words, phrases, and clauses for both the subject and the predicate.

8. Invite students to share their sentences with a partner and then call on several students to share with the entire class.

Often, students can write descriptively in a creative writing class, yet writing descriptively in science, math, or social studies may be even more valuable. Students who can descriptively explain basic science and math processes through writing or describe issues in social studies grow as thinkers and learners in these subject areas.

WRITING STRATEGY 5: SENTENCE COMBINING

Combining sentences helps students understand the relationships relevant to academic writing. Sentence combining asks students to experiment with different ways of putting words and ideas together. Research shows that students expand the size and complexity of their sentences in direct relationship to their progress as a writer (Langer, 2001). The purpose of combining sentences is to create effective, rather than long, sentences. Sentence combining may be the most efficient strategy to help students develop sentence-level maturity in their writing. Research shows sentence combining builds academic language and the relationships of ideas. Searle (2005) notes that

> expressive power builds on the expressive power. You get a snowball effect. So, once the kid gets a few words, that enables him to build more words. Then once he's got more words, he can build more complex sentences. And those more complex sentences enable him to accumulate yet more words. (p. 4)

Combining sentences strengthens students' abilities to construct high-quality sentences. Next, the students should connect the main topics of different paragraphs into essays and longer pieces of writing. Students will become proficient at content-area writing when they effectively use the academic language of actions, relationships, transitions, and concept words.

What Sentence Combining Looks Like

Combining sentences starts small, by joining individual ideas into ever-larger pieces. As students create compound and complex sentences, they make connections between multiple ideas and then integrate these connections into more complex concepts. Combining sentences helps students see that writing is a process of connecting ideas and integrating them into related concepts and expanded meaning. Sentence combining uses academic language transition words to connect sentences and connect relationships between concepts.

Basic Compound Connectors

- And
- Yet
- But
- Or

Complex Connectors

- Not only . . . but also
- Whether . . . or
- Neither . . . nor

- If . . . then
- When . . . then

Additional Complex Connectors

- Because
- In as much
- Since
- However
- Although
- Whenever
- Wherever
- Therefore

Combining With Transitions

Transition language provides the reader with signposts that identify the logical organization of the text. Writing effective transitions help signal the shifts from one idea to the next, one sentence to the next, and one paragraph to the next. Transitions achieve their purposes when they point out common connections between ideas. At other times, transitions achieve their purposes when they effectively emphasize important distinctions. Good writing uses transitions between sentences and between paragraphs to preserve the flow of ideas. Transitions help outline differences for the reader, provide appropriate emphasis, and highlight logical connections. Transition language includes words and phrases that connect ideas between paragraphs. When used in topic sentences, transition language provides clues to the information contained in the upcoming paragraph. Students will find that their concepts build naturally and their writing will progress smoothly as they begin using transitional language terms. Transitions also provide structural clues as to the methods the writer has used to organize the text. Effective transitions support the effective structure of writing, while the effective structure of writing also supports easy transitions. Transition language also reveals relationships between important ideas and combines them within sentences, within paragraphs, and within entire chapters or essays.

Examples of Transition Words and Their Signals

1. The Yankees won the pennant, *and* the peewee Yankees won their neighborhood championship. (Signal: compare/contrast)

2. *If* the equations fail to balance, *then* the equation should be reworked. (Signal: problem-solution)

3. *Whenever* the students finish their assignment, they will get to go outside and play kickball. (Signal: time-order)

4. The croquet ball was hit by an opponent's ball; *therefore* it was knocked off the main field. (Signal: change of direction)

5. *Because* the water reached 212 degrees, it started to boil. (Signal: cause-effect)

Relationship language shows how the upcoming information logically relates to the rest of the topic. Connecting the relationship language to the right arrangement of ideas is an important skill in content-area writing. Some common relationships in content-area writing are *comparisons, contrasts, causes, effects, time sequence, spatial,* and *hierarchical importance.* Whatever type of relationship you want to emphasize and reveal, the academic language is available. Students need practice in combining important relationships within sentences and then correlating these ideas with the main points they want to convey to readers.

How Sentence Combining Works

This strategy works as students develop their ability to combine and connect their ideas together to convey more complex concepts.

1. Share with students that writing is a process of combining sentences and ideas into paragraphs, which connect concepts and convey meaning.

2. Provide students with two separate, yet related, short sentences.

3. Give students a list of transitional relationship words that connect concepts and sentences.

4. Ask students to use transition words to connect the two sentences into one larger, cohesive sentence. Begin with basic connectors, and then move on to more complex connectors.

5. As students demonstrate their ability to combine sentences and connect ideas, give students more challenging assignments, which make more complex relationships.

6. Invite students to share their answers with the class.

7. Over time, you can give students multiple sentences and ask them to combine and organize them into a paragraph or longer essay.

Examples of Combining Sentences

Look over the following examples of pairs of sentences and possible solutions for combining them using academic transition language.

- Lewis and Clark were experienced outdoorsmen.
- They counted on Indian guides like Sacajawea to help them.

   Although Lewis and Clark were experienced outdoorsmen, they counted on Indian guides like Sacajawea to help them.

- Janet put a dollar in the parking meter.
- When she returned three hours later, she had a ticket on her car.

   Janet put a dollar in the parking meter; *however*, when she returned three hours later, she had a ticket on her car.

- Bob opened the can of soda pop.
- The soda sprayed all over his new shirt.

   As Bob opened the can of soda pop, the soda sprayed all over his new shirt.

- Sam likes to go to the ocean.
- The crashing waves on the shore relax his nerves.

   Sam likes to go to the ocean *because* the crashing waves on the shore relax his nerves.

- The experiment comes to a boil.
- The color will change, and the concoction will smell.

   If the experiment comes to a boil, *then* the color will change, and the concoction will smell.

- The architectural plans finally passed.
- We can begin building next week.

   The architectural plans finally passed; *therefore* we can begin building next week.

- The archeologists watched out for looters.
- The archeologists excavated the ancient burial site.

   The archeologists watched out for looters *while* they excavated the ancient burial site.

Mastering the academic language of actions, relationships, transitions, and concepts through consistent classroom practice will dramatically assist students in their quest to become capable writers. Students who are lost and struggle when it comes to writing simple sentences or paragraphs can become proficient through consistent practice. At the same time, students who are proficient will also improve their skills and become more powerful writers.

WRITING STRATEGY 6: COLLABORATIVE WRITING

Collaborative writing is an important component of content-area writing, especially for those students who are reluctant writers or require additional support to engage in writing. The text is negotiated by engaging the students in a prewriting discussion, where it is decided what will be written. Initially, only one sentence of text is negotiated. The teacher shares the recording task, making certain that students record as much as they can—a letter, a part of the word, or a high-frequency word. The goal of the writing is to develop children's independence by encouraging them to use what they already know. Ongoing observations inform the teacher so that each student's strengths can be utilized in the interactive writing session. As the teacher becomes familiar with what individuals already know and can do, every student can contribute to the writing in some way. One student should be selected as scribe to write down the different ideas of the group members. As a warm-up to collaborative writing, the teacher can provide a brief minilesson or teacher write-aloud to focus the students and get their thinking processes working actively. In interactive writing, students collaboratively create writing that is the collective thinking, understanding, and cooperation of the students in the group. Routman (1994) lists several benefits of utilizing the shared writing strategy with students. Some of these include the recognition that collaborative writing

- Reinforces and supports reading as well as writing
- Makes it possible for all students to participate
- Encourages close examination of texts, words, and opinions of authors
- Demonstrates the conventions of writing, spelling, punctuation, and grammar
- Focuses on composing and leaves transcribing to the teacher

Students appreciate that writing can be a shared process rather than a strictly solitary effort.

What Collaborative Writing Looks Like

Collaborative writing may be most beneficial to students who are not yet ready to write independently. The collaborative writing activity can be extremely revealing to teachers, as they see the types of challenges and questions students may have as they proceed through the writing process in a specific content area. Collaborative writing can take several forms. Here are three techniques that can be used to conduct collaborative writing in the classroom.

Three Types of Collaborative Writing

1. Teacher Scribing for Whole-Class Writing
2. Partner Writing
3. Small-Group Composition

Let's take a look at all three types.

Teacher Scribing

The teacher and children collaborate as the whole class composes together. Students are given opportunities to suggest and discuss ideas for the writing process. The teacher, with the pen in hand, involves students in refining ideas before writing what they have composed together.

Partner Writing

The children are given the opportunity to write in a very structured context before they go on to write independently. This usually takes place with the children using mini whiteboards. The teacher monitors their writing and offers support.

Small-Group Composition

Collaborative writing in small groups should be structured to make sure that each student is required to contribute at least one idea to the brainstorming, topic statement development, summarizing, or other aspects of the writing. The teacher should circulate throughout the room and serve as mentor, guiding the groups of students through the writing process.

Students may soon recognize that through consideration and discussion, their collective paper can be clarified and revised to improve the meaning of the message. Language is a shared experience, and sharing the construction of writing can be powerful as students learn to develop their ideas and write collaboratively.

How Collaborative Writing Works

Collaborative Writing

1. Ask students to get in groups of three or four and work collaboratively.
2. Ask students to work together to select a topic.
3. Next, students should work together to select a thesis statement.
4. Students should work together and choose three topic sentences.
5. Students should work together to write an attention grabber.
6. Students should work together to make transitions.
7. Students should work together and decide on at least three supporting details for each paragraph topic.
8. Students then write the essay using powerful action words.
9. Students should then edit, revise, and finish their writing.
10. Invite students to provide a formal presentation of their collaborative writing.
11. Finally, students should provide their own evaluation and assessment of their work.

During shared writing it is important to

- Begin by establishing the purpose for the writing and discuss how this will determine the topic, organization, and main points
- Focus your instruction on one or two specific writing principles or processes that you want your students to learn
- Explain out loud the decisions and choices you make as you write
- Rehearse in your mind the sentences you will write down by saying them before writing
- Encourage and model the habit of inserting proper punctuation as you write

- Constantly reread your writing to help your students determine the flow from one sentence to another
- Stop from time to time and consider out loud other academic language or words that may more precisely convey your message, checking for possible improvements or errors
- Remember to move at a thorough yet appropriate pace to ensure you keep students' attention
- Encourage suggestions from students, checking for misconceptions and providing further explanation
- Make changes from time to time to focus students' attention on specific teaching points

The text that is generated from collaborative writing becomes a recorded document of class activities and learning. This permanent record can be shown to other classes or groups and serves as a student model of writing within the content area. Through collaborative writing, students contribute their own ideas to the content of the text, and they can see that writing is an interactive process of editing, revising, and refining ideas. In time, each individual student will begin to develop their own understanding and confidence in using the process for the various content-area writing assignments.

WRITING STRATEGY 7: SUMMARIZING TEXT

A summary is a consolidated version of a text. It contains the main points in the text and is written in each strudent's own words. It is a mixture of reducing a long text to a short text and selecting relevant information. A good summary shows that you have understood the text. Summaries of written text are valuable indicators that the reader has understood the content conveyed in the text. Students should be given ample opportunities to read the text and then summarize the significant points made by the author. Summaries can synthesize a variety of different texts, yet reading rich, vibrant text makes for more exciting and interesting summaries.

What Summarizing Text Looks Like

Executive summaries of reports are a common method for summarizing information in the business world, while abstracts are common methods for summarizing in college and academic circles. Abstracts summarize and condense the information contained in longer pieces of writing. Abstracts highlight the main ideas and describe the content and scope of the text. The ultimate purpose of summaries is to capture the central message or gist of each text.

Getting the GIST

G et the main idea or central topic

I dentify important information and details

S ummarize the significant impact

T ell others through your writing your understanding

Writing frequent summaries helps to produce great writers because summaries expect the writer to condense the important actions and key concepts into a brief space. Summaries also emphasize the writer's understanding of relevant relationships and smooth transitions. Because summaries are relatively short, writers must become very efficient in identifying and conveying the most important information. Summaries highlight the important actions, key concepts, relevant relationships, and smooth transitions that are vital to powerful academic writing. Summaries should be written in the writer's own words, rather than quoting the text. Summaries help students learn how to write concisely while still conveying the vital information contained in the text.

How Summarizing Text Works

This strategy of summarizing student reading should be practiced and developed on a regular basis. The skill of consolidating information in our mind and summarizing it through writing is an important ability that all of our students should master (adapted from Frey, Fisher, and Hernandez, 2003).

1. First, introduce the text passage, access or build prior knowledge, and frontload key academic language.

2. Explain the four parts of the GIST method as noted above.

3. Next, ask your students to read a passage of text one time through as they consider all four parts of getting the GIST.

4. Students should ask themselves what purposes and points the author wanted to make.

5. Your students should then reread the passage and focus on the introduction and conclusion.

6. They should pause and write down key academic words and important points that they can use in writing their summary.

7. Finally, students should combine the main ideas and supporting details into a one-paragraph summary of five or six sentences. Students should reread their sentences and add transition words if necessary to smooth out the summary.

Through the process of writing summaries, our students will deepen their understanding of a text. As they add their own thinking, while consolidating and concisely organizing the information in their minds, they will become more conversant with the content. Written summaries help our students to infuse their own ideas with the key concepts of a passage, and in the process, they develop greater comprehension and increased ownership of the information.

WRITING STRATEGY 8: EVALUATING ACADEMIC WRITING

Because ideas can be constructed in a multitude of ways, writers need to create sentences that effectively convey the message they intend. Effective academic writers consider a variety of arrangements for their ideas before determining which combination best suits their intended message. Effective writing provides meaning, and sentences flow efficiently while coherently bringing ideas together. Academic writing is essential in preparing students for future learning and occupational opportunities. Effective writing may be the number one skill employers are searching for as they choose those who will lead their organizations.

What Evaluating Academic Writing Looks Like

Evaluating academic writing encompasses the action, transition, and concept language of quality thinking. Consider the following five areas for assessing academic writing.

1. *Clarity.* Does the writing use academic language to precisely convey ideas and accurately describe events?

2. *Voice.* Does the writing use action-oriented words to communicate in active voice and support main ideas and purposes?

3. *Meaning*. Does the writing communicate key ideas effectively and demonstrate relevant relationships that can easily be understood?

4. **Flow.** Does the writing signal key transitions while developing a fluent rhythm?

5. **Organization.** Does the writing connect complex concepts in a logical and organized fashion?

As students evaluate their own writing and the writing of others, they will be able to recognize their strengths and areas for improvement.

How Evaluating Academic Writing Works

This strategy can use a variety of rubrics to help students identify the key principles and processes that will be used to evaluate their writing. I have provided an example of a general writing rubric that emphasizes the importance of academic language in creating effective and powerful writing (see Table 8.1).

Table 8.1 Academic Writing Rubric

	Exemplary (5)	**Proficient (3)**	**Developing (1)**
Clarity	Precise content-area language and academic language used. Very clear thesis connected to great topic sentences.	Appropriate use of specific content-area and academic language. Good thesis and topic sentences.	Little use of specific content-area language or academic language. Thesis and topic sentences unclear.
Voice	Student writing predominantly uses active voice with powerful action verbs. Descriptive language using words, phrases, and clauses helps to provide detail and develop central ideas.	Writing uses passive voice, frequently with helping verbs. Descriptive language primarily uses words and a few phrases to provide detail.	Writing uses weak voice, frequently with linking verbs. Uses only a few descriptive words, providing limited detail.
Meaning	Main ideas and supporting relationships build on one another, and concrete details connect to the topic along with clear commentary, expanding the reader's understanding.	Main ideas receive only a few supporting relationships. Concrete details are loosely connected to the topic, and commentary is off target.	Main ideas are unclear, and supporting relationships are unclear. Concrete details are missing and commentary is unclear.
Flow	The writing effectively uses transition language to signal the organization of the writing. The writing smoothly flows from one point to the next.	Some transition language is used in the writing, yet the writing is somewhat choppy, and the reader may have difficulty smoothly connecting key points together.	No real transitions to signal the organization of the writing. Writing is very choppy and disjointed.
Organization	Writing provides clear examples and connects complex concepts together to create greater meaning and understanding for the reader.	Few examples or weak examples are provided. Concepts are loosely connected, causing readers to grasp little meaning and struggle to understand key points.	No examples are provided, and concepts are disconnected. Main points are scattered, and there is little connection between any supporting information.

[Handwritten margin notes: "Unclear Adjectives in Rubric" and "What's the diff between very clear thesis + good thesis?"]

Evaluating academic writing means much more than just correcting spelling, punctuation, and grammar. Students need to effectively evaluate their own writing and the writing of their peers.

SUMMARY

Developing academic writing is critical to strengthening our students' thinking skills and content-area knowledge. The strategies presented in this chapter prepare students for success in the writing process.

Shared writing helps students see the collaborative nature of writing and supports the processes of refining and synthesizing student thinking. Writing may be the most challenging of the academic literacy practices to master. Great student writing includes both knowledge of content and an understanding of the processes that effectively express ideas. A key component to effective writing in the classroom is to combine sentences. Combining sentences improves students' understanding of the structure of sentences, while it also helps them see transition words more clearly. Summarizing content-area reading can be challenging, yet extremely rewarding. Academic writing improves as students learn to edit language and evaluate the writing of their peers. Writing that uses actions and descriptions creates both moving and colorful images for the audience.

PERSONAL REFLECTIONS

1. Do I provide my students with a variety of content-area writing assignments?

2. How often do I give my students opportunities to work collaboratively on their writing?

3. Are all of my students able to effectively summarize the key actions, relationships, transitions, and concepts in content-area texts?

9 Creating an Academic Culture

Language is the roadmap of a culture. It tells you where its people came from and where they are going.

—Rita Mae Brown, mystery author

ACADEMIC LANGUAGE, LITERACY, AND LEARNING

The path schools should take to achieve success for all students is clearly marked. Integrating academic language into every core-content area will make a major difference in helping learners to see the overlapping expectations of school. Academic language and literacy will open doors and create opportunities for our students. The words our students use in school matter. Consistently engaging learners in academic language in the classroom will dramatically benefit today's students who struggle in school (Scarcella, 2003). Each day, key academic language terms need to be explicitly taught to and learned by students, so that language gaps start to disappear. Students need to develop the content-area language of mathematics, science, social studies, and language arts, which serve as the basic building blocks of school. Along with learning the specific language of core-content disciplines, students also need to learn the general academic language that links curriculum, instruction, and assessment and integrates content-area instruction. The academic language of actions, transitions, and concepts provides the cohesive cement that strengthens each student's ability to access textbooks and classroom standards, while improving their academic literacy. Additionally, successful schools know that at the heart of every educational success story is a process for effectively addressing literacy and language across the curriculum. Literacy is the heart of education, and it provides the lifeblood for instruction. When students can read, write, listen, and speak about important subject matter with skill and precision, then the process of instruction is effectively enhanced. Academic literacy generates the academic pulse that helps all students face the rigors of instruction, build relationships with others, and see relevance in their learning.

ACADEMIC INSTRUCTION

Most important, creating a culture of high-quality instruction is the most significant task that classroom teachers can pursue each and every school day. As academic language becomes part of the instructional culture of a school, then academic literacy and success will develop in every student. Schmoker (2006) calls this type of instruction "authentic literacy," where the culture of schooling integrates language and literacy within content-area instruction. Academic language instruction and literacy practices are critical for English language learners, struggling readers, and students of poverty, so they can close the gaps that exist in their learning. Every educator within their school has a vested interest in improving the instructional processes in academic language and academic literacy. School leaders in the classroom, as well as those that support instruction, need to know where quality results occur, and they need to develop a system for implementing those instructional processes in every classroom. Barber and Mourshed (2007) provide four focus areas where teacher leaders make a difference in academic results.

1. Building practical instructional skills
2. Supporting a coaching model in schools
3. Developing instructional leaders
4. Collaborating with and learning from one another

Effectively integrating academic language instruction throughout the school creates a culture that makes learning a priority. So it is that Cummins (2000) expects that teachers provide "instruction focused on academic language, content, and strategies together with extensive opportunities for students to engage with literacy and collaborative critical inquiry" (p. 268). When academic language and literacy activities are effectively implemented in every classroom and every lesson, then academic results will follow. Our schools can make an impact on student learning in several areas.

Teacher's Impact

1. Provide instruction for all students in general academic language for each grade level.
2. Provide instruction for all students in specific content language as determined by department or grade-level teams.
3. Deliver daily literacy strategies through structured activities in reading, listening, speaking, and writing for every class.
   - *Reading.* Every student should know 90–95% of the academic words in their reading.
   - *Listening.* Every student can acquire new language by following the processes indicated by the seven-step academic language schema.
   - *Speaking.* Every student can engage in content-area conversations that develop academic talk.
   - *Writing.* Every student can use academic language to write coherently and confidently.
4. Integrate academic language skills with academic literacy strategies to develop highly literate learners.
5. Embrace professional development and collaborate and share literacy successes with colleagues.

As you consider how your current professional practices are reaching your students, who do you see needing help to close gaps in their learning? As we remember the stories of Hakim, Mai Xi, Tyrese, Julie, George, Kim, Jennifer, Kathlan, Guillermo, and Jerome from previous chapters, think about how you can impact the story for your school and for your students.

Developing Academic Collaboration

A culture is created when stories and experiences are shared orally or in writing, and they become common stories and common experiences among the individuals in the community. An important part of developing academic language and academic literacy is to create a culture of collaboration regarding instructional practices. Meaningful conversations about instruction by leaders and teachers need to happen on a frequent basis with consistent opportunities to dialogue in-depth as professionals. All teachers can embrace the role of teacher leader at their school by collaborating and sharing their learning experiences. Danielson (2007) emphasizes that "Teacher leaders play a highly significant role in the work of the school and in school improvement efforts. Precisely because of its informal and voluntary nature, teacher leadership represents the highest level of professionalism" (p. 6). Teacher leaders within departments and across grade levels will see that educational processes become efficiently aligned as academic language is explicitly emphasized in the curriculum, instruction, and assessment for each subject area. Through my consulting work, I have helped many schools make a smooth transition to a collaborative culture, while I have seen others without a clear unifying focus struggle to create a community of professionals. Collaborative conversations should center on a culture of reflecting, discussing, and improving instruction.

Professional Learning Protocol

1. Teacher shares an *overview* of an instructional strategy with the professional learning community.

2. Teacher showcases *student evidence.*

3. Allow wait time while peers provide *written feedback.*

4. Discussion and *exchange of ideas* about instructional strategy.

5. Listen to one *suggestion* from each peer.

6. Read written feedback, reflect, and *summarize* ideas.

7. Provide opportunities for peers to observe.

At the conclusion of the collaboration protocol, teachers leave with student evidence, written feedback, and a written summary of what they have learned as a professional. This written documentation keeps collaboration on track and allows others to look over the shared strategies.

Teacher Leader's Impact

1. Model explicit instruction for academic language in classrooms for students and fellow teachers.

2. Collaboratively develop the specific content-area language lists in each discipline for each grade level.

3. Support the delivery of literacy strategies by helping all content-area teachers improve literacy practices.

4. Observe and encourage fellow teachers on the integration of academic language and academic literacy.

5. Lead collaboration meetings and share important literacy lessons learned in the classroom.

6. Embrace professional development and training opportunities.

Teachers as instructional leaders can set the tone and provide an example for students as they demonstrate their commitment to truly develop a community of learners. When teachers and leaders speak, listen, read, and write collaboratively about their own instructional practices, they can create a culture of consistent school improvement. As teachers and administrators learn to collaborate together, instruction can improve across grade levels and throughout content areas. Reducing the achievement gap will take a coordinated and collaborative effort by everyone in the school. As teachers share their experiences with instructional strategies and coordinate their efforts around the language of school, college, and career, they will see consistent improvement in student learning.

CREATING AN ACADEMIC CULTURE

Each educator's goal should be to create a culture of literacy on the campus, in the classroom, and within each learner. Creating a culture of academic literacy will require cooperation and collaboration at several levels. Thus, Phillips (2005) acknowledges, "Strong leadership from both administrators and teachers is an essential building block in constructing a successful literacy program, but the role played by the principal is key to determining success or failure of the program" (p. 7). The school principal can help create an academic culture by making the school library the hub of the campus. Libraries provide lots of books, magazines, and resources that send a clear message to students about the importance of words, reading, and learning. Schools that make the library an inviting place to hang out send a powerful signal that literacy is essential to success. As schools emphasize an academic culture in every classroom, the library can stand as a gathering place and symbol of literacy and learning. As resistance to collaboration is overcome, a more cooperative culture will develop and students ultimately benefit. The achievement gap can be bridged for our students if we collectively target the academic language of curriculum, instruction, and assessment.

Site Administrator's Impact

1. Provide professional development in academic language and literacy that provides definitional clarity and a core foundation for schoolwide efforts.

2. Support the implementation of instruction that provides all students a targeted, strategic approach to overcoming language and literacy gaps.

3. Develop collaborative teams or professional learning communities to support instructional capacity building throughout the school.

4. Staff the school library during lunch and before and after school so it can become the hub of the school.

5. Provide the library with magazines, books, computers, and resources to engage students.

6. Work with the district to coordinate professional development and collaboration within the school.

Site administrators will appreciate the benefits that accrue as students recognize that academic language is integrated in various content areas and classrooms. Everyone benefits when a culture of collaboration is created across the campus and throughout the district.

STRENGTHENING ACADEMIC LEADERSHIP

Educational leaders who provide academic leadership help their school develop a common professional language, share productive experiences, embrace professional development, and celebrate their successes. Wong-Fillmore (2007) points out that "Both site and district administrators have to work closely with teachers in making thoughtful curriculum and instruction decisions in support of academic language learning. They also need to support teachers as they incorporate these strategies into the classroom" (p. 6). Creating a culture of collaboration in education requires that individuals share their understanding and experiences with each other. Schools that have created an academic culture through professional learning have developed

- A widely shared sense of purpose and values
- Norms of continuous learning and improvement
- A commitment to and sense of responsibility for the learning of all students
- Collaborative and collegial relationships
- Opportunities for staff reflection, collective inquiry, and sharing personal practice (adapted from Fullan, 2003)

It is important for teachers to reflect on their own educational efforts and observe the learning culture that is provided by their peers. A culture of collaboration focuses the conversation and professional dialogue on the actual instructional practices that affect students and student learning. Successful educational collaboration revolves around listening, speaking, reading, writing, and particularly around viewing the instructional quality that surrounds the central purposes of education.

District Administrator's Impact

1. Support the implementation of instructional practices by academic language at each grade level and in every core subject while also developing the personal strategies and abilities to become life-long, highly literate learners.

2. Increase instructional capacity by establishing collaboration time, where teachers can share their effective academic language and literacy practices with one another.

3. Improve sustainability by supporting a culture of literacy for all students.

4. Provide professional development opportunities in content-area literacy for each school.

Collaborative results need a powerful purpose to engage the sustained efforts of key players in teaching, instruction, and learning. Site-level administrators need to enlist the energies and ideas of teachers who can lead instruction and learning results to even higher levels for all students. When collaboration supports administrators and teachers as instructional leaders, who reflect on instructional activities, practices, and strategies, then a professional atmosphere of proven results will prevail.

DEVELOPING PROFESSIONALLY

Supporting and sustaining a strong culture of professional development is an important task for all school leaders. Elmore (2002) emphasizes, "In summary, the practice of improvement is largely about moving whole organizations—teachers, administrators, and schools—toward the culture, structure, norms, and processes that support quality professional development in the service of student learning" (p. 15). Professional development in language and learning will help each teacher and administrator understand the strategies that will allow everyone to take effective action. Constas and Sternberg (2006) note in their research that instructional strategies in literacy supported by professional development

> have proven effective for students, especially those who arrive at school lacking fluency in academic language. Professional development strategies, where these can be implemented for a sustained amount of time, appear to lead to fundamental changes for teachers.

Bielenberg and Wong-Fillmore (2005) encourage school leaders to improve academic results by recognizing "the role that academic English plays in test performance and classroom learning and by encouraging and providing opportunities for all teachers to participate in professional development activities that address this issue" (p. 49). Professional development in language and literacy will definitely help build capacity and improve learning for all students. Through professional development in academic language and literacy, you can develop an academic foundation and framework for building success at your school.

SUMMARY

Let me wrap up the book by telling you—Thank You! By reading *Academic Language! Academic Literacy!* you have engaged in a conversation that directly affects our profession. The impact you make in your students' lives deserves to be celebrated. I hope you will continue to engage in the academic discourse at your school and connect with your fellow educators who value academic literacy. As we collaboratively share our insights with our colleagues, it will go a long way toward creating a culture of academic achievement. I would love to hear about the progress you are making as you improve academic language and literacy for your students. If you need help integrating academic language instruction into your schools or you would appreciate help developing as a professional learning community, please contact me (eli@achievement4all.com). Also, feel free to share both the challenges and successes you are currently experiencing. Ultimately, this book is about your story and the language and literacy that your students acquire in their pursuit for academic success. May the story of your classroom and your school be one of enriched language, literacy, and learning for every student!

PERSONAL REFLECTIONS

1. What strategies will you implement in your classroom to make sure every student receives daily practice in academic language?

2. How will you support professional development in academic language at your school to improve instructional capacity?

3. What is your action plan for developing sustainability at your school to improve academic literacy for every student?

Resource A

Academic Language Grade-Level Lists

KINDERGARTEN

1. Act
2. Add
3. After
4. Aid
5. Always
6. Answer
7. Apply
8. Ask
9. Before
10. Build
11. But
12. Care
13. Chart
14. Choose
15. Collect
16. Compare
17. Decrease
18. Differ
19. Equal
20. Find
21. Finish
22. Fix
23. Focus
24. Gather
25. Get
26. Give
27. Go
28. Goal
29. Group
30. Guess
31. Help
32. How
33. If
34. Include
35. Join
36. Know
37. Label
38. Like
39. Link
40. List
41. Listen
42. Make
43. Minus
44. Never
45. Order
46. Plus
47. Prepare
48. Print
49. Question
50. Read
51. Role
52. Rule
53. Same
54. Save
55. Say
56. Sense
57. Share
58. Show
59. Speak
60. Subtract
61. Support
62. Task
63. Team
64. Tell
65. Test
66. Think
67. Understand
68. View
69. What
70. When
71. Where
72. Who
73. Why
74. Work
75. Write

FIRST GRADE

1. Again
2. Aid
3. Almost
4. Another
5. Appreciate
6. Aware
7. Because
8. Check
9. Collect
10. Combine
11. Community
12. Contrast
13. Control
14. Cooperate
15. Define
16. Deliver
17. Describe
18. Different
19. Discuss
20. During

21. Earlier
22. Earn
23. Educate
24. Emotional
25. Encourage
26. Energy
27. Explain
28. Finally
29. Gather
30. Greet
31. Grow
32. Guide
33. Highlight
34. Hire
35. Idea
36. Identify
37. Infer
38. Instruct
39. Involve
40. Know
41. Language
42. Later
43. Learn
44. Locate
45. Meet
46. Memorize
47. Mental
48. Nearly
49. Next
50. Now
51. Part
52. Pattern
53. Physical
54. Place
55. Practice
56. Preview
57. Primary
58. Prior
59. Proceed
60. Progress
61. Rate
62. Recall
63. Report
64. Reverse
65. Review
66. Similar
67. Since
68. Soon
69. Study
70. Suggest
71. Target
72. Then
73. Unlike
74. Weigh
75. Yet

SECOND GRADE

1. Accept
2. Adapt
3. Almost
4. Also
5. Another
6. Arrange
7. Assess
8. Assign
9. Attract
10. Author
11. Balance
12. Behave
13. Beyond
14. Categorize
15. Chapter
16. Compare
17. Compete
18. Complete
19. Connect
20. Consider
21. Control
22. Cooperate
23. Crack
24. Design
25. Direct
26. Discipline
27. Edit
28. Educate
29. Encourage
30. Environment
31. Expert
32. External
33. Finally
34. Follow
35. Formula
36. General
37. Government
38. Inquire
39. Internal
40. Judge
41. Maybe
42. Measure
43. Nature
44. Negative
45. Neutral
46. Norm
47. Nurture
48. Objective
49. Occupation
50. Opinion
51. Option
52. Outcome
53. Participate
54. Persist
55. Positive
56. Possible
57. Power
58. Present
59. Probably
60. Proceed
61. Process
62. Purpose
63. Resource
64. Responsibility
65. Scan
66. Secondary
67. Select
68. Set up
69. So
70. Social
71. Summarize
72. Support
73. Target
74. Topic
75. Unity

THIRD GRADE

1. Academic
2. Achieve
3. As
4. Assemble
5. Assess
6. Attitude
7. Attribute
8. Award
9. Balance
10. Believe
11. Bias
12. Chart
13. Clarify
14. Code
15. Communicate
16. Concept

17. Confidence
18. Control
19. Core
20. Cycle
21. Data
22. Decision
23. Demonstrate
24. Despite
25. Detect
26. Elect
27. Emotional
28. Employ
29. Eventually
30. Exercise
31. Experiment

32. Explore
33. Foundation
34. Frequently
35. Global
36. Grant
37. Immediately
38. Instead
39. Integrate
40. Intelligence
41. Introduce
42. Invite
43. Level
44. Mental
45. Method
46. Model

47. Objectives
48. Organize
49. Perhaps
50. Phase
51. Portfolio
52. Primary
53. Profession
54. Project
55. Publish
56. Punish
57. Quality
58. Quantity
59. Reflect
60. Region
61. Report

62. Self-control
63. Settle
64. Sketch
65. Social
66. Source
67. Supply
68. System
69. Theme
70. Train
71. Transport
72. Trend
73. Tutor
74. Until
75. While

FOURTH GRADE

1. Additionally
2. Adjust
3. Afterwards
4. Anticipate
5. Apply
6. Approve
7. Assist
8. Attitude
9. Authority
10. Character
11. College
12. Concept
13. Conserve
14. Culture
15. Curriculum
16. Defend
17. Devote
18. Dialogue
19. Document

20. Eliminate
21. Emphasize
22. Equality
23. Evaluate
24. Evidence
25. Examine
26. Exchange
27. Exercise
28. Exhibit
29. Express
30. Feedback
31. Fine-tune
32. For example
33. Frame
34. Frequently
35. Gauge
36. Host
37. Importantly
38. Inform

39. Inspire
40. Lecture
41. License
42. Lighten
43. Log
44. Mean
45. Mention
46. Motivate
47. Nurture
48. Operate
49. Portfolio
50. Prevent
51. Principles
52. Produce
53. Range
54. Rather
55. Reality
56. Reason
57. Reduce

58. Relate
59. Release
60. Replace
61. Represent
62. Research
63. Result
64. Retain
65. Schedule
66. Signify
67. Similarly
68. Sometimes
69. Stimulate
70. Strengthen
71. Structure
72. Supervise
73. Technology
74. Translate
75. Update

FIFTH GRADE

1. Approach
2. Automatically
3. Besides
4. Bias

5. Challenge
6. Collaborate
7. Collate
8. Commit

9. Compile
10. Conclude
11. Conduct
12. Conscious

13. Consequence
14. Content
15. Enable
16. Engage

17. Environment
18. Equip
19. Establish
20. Even though
21. Ever Since
22. Expand
23. Expert
24. Explain
25. Extend
26. Feature
27. Fee
28. Forecast
29. Furthermore
30. In order that
31. Influence
32. Inspect
33. Install
34. Insure
35. Involve
36. Issue
37. Launch
38. Maintain
39. Manage
40. Maximize
41. Meanwhile
42. Medical
43. Narrate
44. Navigate
45. On the other hand
46. Opinion
47. Perfect
48. Preserve
49. Primarily
50. Probability
51. Reason
52. Refine
53. Remodel
54. Repair
55. Reserve
56. Respond
57. Restrict
58. Retain
59. Sample
60. Screen
61. Series
62. Simplify
63. Still
64. Straighten
65. Submit
66. Surely
67. Symbolic
68. Synthesize
69. System
70. Technical
71. Thus
72. Transform
73. Uncover
74. Unify
75. Upgrade

SIXTH GRADE

1. Abstract
2. Accumulate
3. Assume
4. Boost
5. Career
6. Certainly
7. Cite
8. Civil
9. Clause
10. Component
11. Conceptualize
12. Concrete
13. Console
14. Contact
15. Contrastingly
16. Currently
17. Dedicate
18. Defer
19. Diagnose
20. Differentiate
21. Discharge
22. Effective
23. Efficient
24. Enlarge
25. Enlist
26. Even when
27. Expand
28. Extract
29. File
30. Filter
31. Finalize
32. Habit
33. Initially
34. Institute
35. Integrate
36. Likelihood
37. Localize
38. Logic
39. Mediate
40. Mentor
41. Merge
42. Metaphor
43. Modify
44. Moral
45. Notify
46. Obtain
47. Occupation
48. Perceive
49. Perhaps
50. Preside
51. Reaction
52. Reference
53. Regulate
54. Relevance
55. Reorganize
56. Response
57. Restore
58. Scheme
59. Scope
60. Sequentially
61. Significantly
62. Simultaneously
63. Spearhead
64. Specialize
65. Survey
66. Tense
67. Therefore
68. Transfer
69. Transmit
70. Undertake
71. Unveil
72. Value
73. Version
74. Viewpoint
75. Witness

SEVENTH GRADE

1. Adapt
2. Allocate
3. Although
4. Analogy
5. Appoint
6. As a result
7. Awareness
8. Coincidentally
9. Comment
10. Contend
11. Correspond
12. Counsel

13. Criteria
14. Cultivate
15. Customize
16. Disclose
17. Dispatch
18. Diversify
19. Element
20. Enforce
21. Engineer
22. Enhance
23. Enrich
24. Ensure
25. Eventually
26. Fabricate
27. For instance
28. Formulate
29. Fortify
30. Framework
31. Further
32. Furthermore
33. Illustrate
34. Impart
35. In spite of
36. Indeed
37. Initiate
38. Insight
39. Integrity
40. Intermediate
41. Intervene
42. Justify
43. Likewise
44. Mean
45. Median
46. Minimize
47. Minority
48. Mobilize
49. Mode
50. Moderate
51. Moreover
52. Mutual
53. Nonetheless
54. Officiate
55. Prioritize
56. Probe
57. Rehabilitate
58. Reinforce
59. Retain
60. Retrieve
61. Revise
62. Specify
63. Sphere
64. Stability
65. Strategy
66. Surpass
67. Sustain
68. Technique
69. Therefore
70. Transform
71. Upheld
72. Vary
73. Vitalize
74. Whereby
75. Withdraw

EIGHTH GRADE

1. Affect
2. Amend
3. Analogy
4. Annually
5. Anticipate
6. Appraise
7. Aspect
8. Assure
9. Attain
10. Benefit
11. Broaden
12. Characteristic
13. Circumstance
14. Commodity
15. Confer
16. Conform
17. Consult
18. Context
19. Controversy
20. Conversely
21. Criteria
22. Devote
23. Dimension
24. Dissect
25. Domain
26. Doubtless
27. Element
28. Enlighten
29. Enumerate
30. Ethics
31. Facilitate
32. Familiarize
33. Federal
34. Flexibility
35. Foster
36. Fundamental
37. Hypothesis
38. Identical
39. Import
40. Improvise
41. Incorporate
42. Individualize
43. Initially
44. Innovate
45. Issue
46. Just as
47. Literacy
48. Meantime
49. Modify
50. Nevertheless
51. Notion
52. Offset
53. Opposing
54. Overall
55. Overhaul
56. Perspective
57. Phenomenon
58. Philosophy
59. Policy
60. Promote
61. Regardless
62. Render
63. Resolve
64. Retain
65. Scenario
66. Secure
67. Segment
68. Simulate
69. Statistic
70. Status
71. Subsequently
72. Thesis
73. Though
74. Variable
75. Visualize

NINTH GRADE

1. Abstract
2. Accommodate
3. Accordingly
4. Adequate
5. Align
6. Anticipate
7. Attain
8. Capacity
9. Chemical
10. Classical
11. Compatible
12. Comprise

13. Condense
14. Confirm
15. Contrarily
16. Conversely
17. Convert
18. Despite
19. Domestic
20. Dynamic
21. Eliminate
22. Erode
23. Estate
24. Explicit
25. Formulate
26. Function
27. Generalize
28. Guarantee
29. Harmonize
30. Hierarchy
31. However
32. Hypothesis
33. Implicit
34. Incorporate
35. Infinite
36. Infrastructure
37. Insight
38. Instance
39. Interpret
40. Investigate
41. Likewise
42. Mature
43. Meanwhile
44. Nonetheless
45. Orchestrate
46. Oversee
47. Parameter
48. Partnership
49. Portion
50. Practitioner
51. Precede
52. Propose
53. Protocol
54. Publicize
55. Randomly
56. Relevance
57. Reluctantly
58. Revitalize
59. Revolution
60. Satisfy
61. Somewhat
62. Standardize
63. Streamline
64. Stress
65. Successively
66. Symbolize
67. Synthesize
68. Temporarily
69. Tendency
70. Terminology
71. Terms
72. Theory
73. Thereby
74. Ultimately
75. Vitalize

TENTH GRADE

1. Accelerate
2. Accordingly
3. Accumulate
4. Activate
5. Advise
6. Advocate
7. Affirm
8. Allocate
9. Appreciate
10. Arbitrate
11. Ascertain
12. Audit
13. Auditory
14. Augment
15. Avert
16. Bolster
17. Calibrate
18. Catalogue
19. Cater
20. Centralize
21. Cheer
22. Consider
23. Consolidate
24. Crucial
25. Debate
26. Depict
27. Depreciate
28. Derive
29. Devote
30. Differentiate
31. Disseminate
32. Dramatize
33. Elicit
34. Enrich
35. Envision
36. Excite
37. Exert
38. Extend
39. Extrapolate
40. Figurative
41. Foregoing
42. Hence
43. Ideology
44. Implement
45. Interface
46. Interpersonal
47. Literal
48. Litigate
49. Median
50. Metacognition
51. Mislead
52. Mode
53. Nevertheless
54. Nuance
55. Oppose
56. Orbit
57. Paraphrase
58. Perspective
59. Recap
60. Recommend
61. Retract
62. Revamp
63. Rubric
64. Scheme
65. Scrutinize
66. Simulation
67. Strategize
68. Systematize
69. Tabulate
70. Transcribe
71. Transpose
72. Troubleshoot
73. Trust
74. Verbal
75. Widespread

ELEVENTH GRADE

1. Accompany
2. Acknowledge
3. Administrate
4. Advocate
5. Apparent
6. Aspect
7. Authentic
8. Behalf
9. Cherish
10. Commence
11. Compensate
12. Comprehensive

13. Conceive
14. Confer
15. Consent
16. Consist
17. Constitute
18. Continuity
19. Contradict
20. Converse
21. Crucial
22. Deconstruct
23. Deduce
24. Despite
25. Deviate
26. Discrepancy
27. Discriminate
28. Displace
29. Distinct
30. Enforce
31. Explicit
32. Fluctuate
33. Forecast
34. Format
35. Forthcoming
36. Generate
37. Guideline
38. Ideology
39. Ignorance
40. Implicit
41. Impose
42. Incidence
43. Incorporate
44. Index
45. Infrastructure
46. Inherent
47. Inherit
48. Initiate
49. Innovate
50. Integral
51. Intensity
52. Intervene
53. Isolate
54. Maximize
55. Minimize
56. Negate
57. Orient
58. Perceive
59. Perspective
60. Precede
61. Refine
62. Regulate
63. Resolve
64. Restrain
65. Reveal
66. Scrutinize
67. So-called
68. Somewhat
69. Specify
70. Sufficient
71. Supplement
72. Transmit
73. Undergo
74. Utilize
75. Violate

TWELFTH GRADE

1. Accessorize
2. Accommodate
3. Albeit
4. Ambiguous
5. Append
6. Appropriate
7. Arbitrary
8. Assimilate
9. Calibrate
10. Cohere
11. Coherent
12. Coincide
13. Compute
14. Conciliate
15. Concurrent
16. Connote
17. Conscience
18. Constitute
19. Construct
20. Contact
21. Contemporary
22. Controversy
23. Convene
24. Criticize
25. Denotation
26. Denote
27. Discrete
28. Dismantle
29. Dominate
30. Duration
31. Elicit
32. Empirical
33. Encounter
34. Entity
35. Ethic
36. Excerpt
37. Exclude
38. Extrapolate
39. Henceforth
40. Implication
41. Imply
42. Incentive
43. Incline
44. Inevitably
45. Inherent
46. Institute
47. Isolate
48. Kinesthetic
49. Linguistic
50. Liquidate
51. Meta-Analysis
52. Notwithstanding
53. Orientate
54. Paradigm
55. Phenomenon
56. Preliminarily
57. Probable
58. Protocol
59. Pseudo
60. Ramification
61. Repertoire
62. Scene
63. Speculate
64. Supplement
65. Surmise
66. Syntax
67. Synthesize
68. Tabulate
69. Tactile
70. Tangent
71. Terminate
72. Transparent
73. Underlie
74. Virtual
75. Whereby

Resource B

Specific Content Language Resources

In addition to the Academic Language Grade Level Lists (Resource A), teachers should develop their own specific content-area word lists for each grade level. Listed below are several resources that have already developed example lists. The resources listed should serve as a starting point. In addition to using these lists, content-area teachers can use state standards, textbook vocabulary, and other resources to develop their own specific content-area word lists. The science and social studies resources provide access to lists with 75 words for each grade level provided in nine different languages.

Science. http://www.lacoe.edu/includes/templates/document_frame.cfm?toURL=documents&id=5707

Social Studies. http://history.ocde.us/Instructional_Materials_and_Adoption.htm

Mathematics and Music. http://www.uefap.com/vocab/vocfram.htm

Language Arts. http://www.dowlingcentral.com/MrsD/area/studyguides/Languageterms.htm

References

Adams, M. (1990). *Beginning to read: Thinking and learning in print.* Cambridge: MIT Press.

Alfasi, M. (2004). Reading to learn: Effects of combined strategy instruction on high school students. *The Journal of Educational Research, 97,* 171–184.

Alliance for Education. (n.d.). *About the crisis.* Retrieved April 05, 2009, from http://www.all4ed.org/about_the_crisis

Anderson, R. C. (1992). *Research foundations for wide reading.* Paper commissioned by the World Bank. Urbana, IL: Center for the Study of Reading.

Anderson-Hsieh, J., & Koehler, K. (1988). The effect of foreign accent and speaking rate on native speaker comprehension. *Language Learning, 38,* 561–613.

Applebee, A., Langer, J., Nystrand, M., & Gamoran, A. (2003). Discussion-based approaches to developing understanding: Classroom instruction and student performance in middle and high school English. *American Education Research Journal, 40*(3), 685–730.

August, D., & Shanahan, T. (Eds.). (2006). *Developing literacy in second-language learners: Report of the National Literacy Panel on Language-Minority Children and Youth.* Mahwah, NJ: Lawrence Erlbaum.

Bailey, A. (2007). *The language demands of school: Putting academic English to the test.* New Haven, CT: Yale University Press.

Bailey, A., & Butler, F. (2003). An evidentiary framework for operationalizing academic language for broad application to K–12 education: A design document. Los Angeles, CA: CRESST.

Bailey, A., Butler, F., Laframenta, C., & Ong, C. (2004). Towards the characterization of academic language in upper elementary science classrooms: CSE Report 621. Los Angeles, CA: CRESST.

Ballard & Tighe. (2007). *Academic language.* Retrieved March 19, 2009, from http://www.nclb.ballard-tighe.com/research/academic.html

Barber, M., & Mourshed, M. (2007, September). *How the world's best-performing school systems come out on top.* McKinsey & Company. Retrieved March 19, 2009, from www.mckinsey.com/clientservice/socialsector/resources/pdf/Worlds_School_Systems_Final.pdf

Barton, P. (2003). *Parsing the achievement gap: Baselines for tracking progress.* Princeton, NJ: Educational Testing Services.

Baugh, J. (2000). *Beyond Ebonics: Linguistic pride and racial prejudice.* New York: Oxford University Press.

Beck, I., & McKeown, M. (2004, January). Increasing young low-income children's oral vocabulary repertoires through rich and focused instruction. *Elementary School Journal, 107*(3), 251–273.

Beck, I., McKeown, M., & Kucan, L. (2002). *Bringing words to life: Robust vocabulary instruction.* New York: Guilford Press.

Beers, K. (2003). *When kids can't read: What teachers can do about it.* Portsmouth, NH: Heinemann.

Beier, M., & Ackerman, P. (2005). Working memory and intelligence: Different constructs. *Psychological Bulletin, 131,* 72–75.

Bell, L. (2003). Strategies that close the gap. *Educational Leadership, 60*(4), 32–34.

Bielenberg, B., & Wong-Fillmore, L. (2005). The English they need for the test. *Educational Leadership, 62*(4), 45–49.

Braunger, J., & Lewis, J. (2005). *Building a knowledge base in reading* (2nd ed.). Newark, DE: International Reading Association.

Brisk, M. (2005). Bilingual education. In Eli Hinkel (Ed.), *Handbook of research in second language teaching and learning* (pp. 7–24). Mahwah, NJ: Lawrence Erlbaum Associates.

Cain, K., & Oakhill, J. (2007). *Children's comprehension problems in oral and written languages.* New York: Guilford Press.

Calderon, M. (2007). *Teaching reading to English language learners, grades 6–12: A framework for improving achievement in the content areas.* Thousand Oaks, CA: Corwin.

California Department of Education. (2004). *Science framework for California public schools: Kindergarten through grade twelve.* Sacramento, CA: Author.

Carnevale, A. (2001). *Help wanted . . . college required.* Washington, DC: Educational Testing Service, Office for Public Leadership.

Carrasquillo, A. L., & Rodriguez, V. (2002). *Language minority students in the mainstream classroom* (2nd ed.). Clevedon, UK: Multilingual Matters.

Cazden, C. (1988). *Classroom discourse: The language of teaching and learning.* Portsmouth, NH: Heinemann.

Chamot, A., & O'Malley, J. (1994). *The CALLA handbook: Implementing the cognitive academic language learning approach.* White Plains, NY: Addison Wesley.

Chaudron, C., & Richards, J. (1986). The effect of discourse markers on the comprehension of lectures. *Applied Linguistics, 7*(2), 113–127.

Christie, F. (1985). Language and schooling. In S. Tchudi (Ed.), *Language, schooling, and society* (pp. 21–40). Upper Montclair, NJ: Noynton/Cook.

Coleman, J. S. (1990). *Equality and achievement in education.* San Francisco: Westview.

Constas, M., & Sternberg, R. (2006). *Translating theory and research into educational practice.* Mahwah, NJ: Lawrence Erlbaum.

Cosby, B., & Poussaint, A. (2007). *Come on, people: On the path from victims to victors.* Nashville, TN: Thomas Nelson.

Costa, A., & Kallick, B. (2000). *Habits of mind. A developmental series.* Alexandria, VA: Association for Supervision and Curriculum Development.

Crary, D. (2008). *Report: Percentage of U.S. babies with low birth weights is highest in 40 years.* New York: Associated Press.

Crow, T. (2008). Practicing professionals: Q&A with R. Elmore. *National Staff Development Council, 29*(2), 46.

Cummins, J. (2000). *Language, power, and pedagogy: Bilingual children in the crossfire.* Clevedon, England: Multilingual Matters.

Cunningham, A. E., & Stanovich, K. E. (1998). What reading does for the mind. *American Educator, 22*(2), 8–15.

Dale, E., & O'Rourke, J. (1986). *Vocabulary building.* Columbus, OH: Zaner-Bloser.

Danielson. C. (2007). *Enhancing professional practice: A framework for teaching* (2nd ed.). Alexandria, VA: Association for Supervision and Curriculum Development.

DeCarrico, J., & Nattinger, J. (1988). Lexical phrases and the comprehension of academic lectures. *English for Specific Purposes, 7,* 91–102.

Dickson, S. V., Simmons, D. C., & Kame'enui, E. J. (1995). *Text organization: Curricular and instructional implications for diverse learners* (Technical Report No. 18). Eugene, OR: National Center to Improve the Tools of Educators.

Drake, S. (2007). *Creating standards-based integrated curriculum: Aligning curriculum, content, assessment, and instruction.* Thousand Oaks, CA: Corwin.

Dunkel, P. (1993). *Listening in the native and second/foreign language: Toward an integration of research and practice.* Washington, DC: TESOL.

Earle, L., Watson, N., Levin, B., Leithwood, K., Fullan, M., & Torrance, N. (2003). *Watching and learning 3. Evaluation of England's national literacy and numeracy strategies, third and final report.* Toronto, Ontario, Canada: Ontario Institute for Studies in Education, University of Toronto.

Elmore, R. (2002). *Bridging the gap between standards and achievement.* Washington, DC: Albert Shanker Institute.

Fearn, L., & Farnan, N. (2005, April). *An investigation of the influence of teaching grammar in writing to accomplish an influence on writing.* Paper presented at the annual meeting of the American Educational Research Association, Montreal, Canada.

Feldman, K., & Kinsella, K. (2005). *Narrowing the language gap: The case for explicit vocabulary instruction.* New York: Scholastic.

Fielding, L., Kerr, N., & Rosier, P. (2007). *Annual growth, catch-up growth.* Kennewick, WA: New Foundation Press.

Fisher, D., & Frey, N. (2008). *Better learning through structured teaching: A framework for the gradual release of responsibility.* Alexandria, VA: ASCD.

Francis, D., Rivera, M., Lesaux, N., Kieffer, M., & Rivera, H. (2006). *Practical guidelines for the education of English language learners: Research-based recommendations for instruction and academic interventions.* Portsmouth, NH: RMC Research Corporation, Center on Instruction.

Frank, D. (2001). *Focus on Physical Science.* New York: Pearson Prentice Hall.

Franklin Institute. (n.d.). *Statesman.* Retrieved March 27, 2009, from www.fi.edu/franklin/statsman/statsman.html

Frey, N., Fisher, D., & Hernandez, T. (2003). What's the gist? Summary writing for struggling adolescent writers. *Voices from the Middle, 11*(2), 43–49.

Fullan, M. (2003). *The moral imperative of school leadership.* Thousand Oaks, CA: Corwin.

Fullan, M. (2007). *Foreword in the literacy principal: Leading, supporting, and assessing reading and writing initiatives* (2nd ed.). Portland, ME: Pembroke.

Gee, J. (2001). *Language in the science classroom: Academic social languages as the heart of school-based literacy.* Paper presented at Crossing Borders: Connecting Science and Literacy Conference, Sponsored by National Science Foundation and The Elementary Science Integration Projects, Baltimore, MD.

Gernsbacher, M., Varner, K., & Faust, M. (1990). Investigating individual differences in general comprehension skill. *Journal of Experimental Psychology: Learning, Memory, and Cognition, 16,* 430–445.

Gersten, R., Baker, S., Shanahan, T., Linan-Thompson, S., Collins, P., and Scarcella, R. (2007). *Effective literacy and English language instruction for English learners in the elementary grades.* Washington, DC: Institute of Education Sciences, U.S. Department of Education.

Gibbons, P. (2002). *Scaffolding language, scaffolding learning: Teaching second language learners in the mainstream classroom.* Portsmouth, NH: Heinemann.

Gopen, G., & Swan, J. (1990, November–December). The science of scientific writing. *American Scientist, 78,* 550–558.

Gough, P., & Tunmer, W. (1986). Decoding, reading, and reading disability. *Remedial and Special Education, 7*(1), 6–10.

Graham, S., & Perin, D. (2007). *Writing Next: Effective strategies to improve writing of adolescents in middle and high schools.* Washington, DC: Alliance for Excellent Education.

Halliday, M. (1994). *An introduction to systemic functional linguistics.* London: Pinter.

Hambrick, D., & Oswald, F. (2005). Does domain knowledge moderate involvement of working memory capacity in higher-level cognition? A test of three models. *Journal of Memory and Language, 52,* 377–397.

Hart, B., & Risley, T. (2003, Spring). The early catastrophe: The 30 million word gap by age 3. *American Educator, 27*(1), 4–9.

Harvey, S., & Goudvis, A. (2007). *Strategies that work: Teaching comprehension for understanding and engagement.* Portland, ME: Stenhouse.

Hayes, D. P., & Ahrens, M. (1988). Speaking and writing: Distinct patterns of word choice. *Journal of Memory and Language, 27,* 572–585.

Haynes, J. (2006). *Getting started with English language learners: How educators can meet the challenge.* Alexandria, VA: Association for Supervision and Curriculum Development.

Heller, R., & Greenleaf, C. (2007). *Literacy instruction in the content areas: Getting to the core of middle and high school improvement.* Washington, DC: Alliance for Excellent Education.

Henrichs, L. (2006). Schooltaalvaardigheid operationaliseren: de ontwikkeling van een coderingsschema binnen het DASH-project [School proficiency operational lists: For the development of a coding outline within the DASH project]. In T. Koole, J. Nortier, & B. Tahitu (Eds.), *Artikelen vande Vijfde sociolinguïstische conferentie* [Fifth Sociolinguistic Conference] (pp. 246–256). Delft, The Netherlands: Eburon.

Hiebert, F., & Kamil, M. (2005). *Teaching and learning vocabulary.* Mahwah, NJ: Lawrence Erlbaum.

Hinkel, E. (2005). *Handbook of research in second language teaching and learning.* Mahwah, NJ: Lawrence Erlbaum.

Hirsch, E. (2003, Spring). Reading comprehension requires knowledge of words and the world: Scientific insights into the fourth-grade slump and the nation's stagnant comprehension scores. *American Educator, 27*(1), 10–29.

Hirsch, E. (2006, Spring). The case for bringing content into the language arts block and for a knowledge-rich curriculum core for all children. *American Educator, 30*(1), 8–17.

Honig, B., Diamond, L., & Gutlohn, L. (2000). *Teaching reading: Sourcebook for kindergarten through eighth grade.* Novato, CA: Arena Press.

Hu, W. (2008, March 23). Glimmers of progress at a failing school. *New York Times.* Retrieved March 22, 2009, from http://www.nytimes.com/2008/03/23/nyregion/nyregionspecial2/23Rnewark.html?ref=education

Irvin, J., Meltzer, J., & Dukes, M. (2007). *Taking action on adolescent literacy.* Alexandria, VA: Association of Supervision and Curriculum Development.

Jacobs, H. (2006). *Active literacy across the curriculum.* Larchmont. New York: Eye on Education.

Juel, C. (2008). *Keys to early reading success: Word recognition and meaning vocabulary.* Glenview, IL: Pearson Scott-Foresman.

Kame'enui, E., & Carnine, D. (1998). *Effective teaching strategies that accommodate diverse learners.* New York: Prentice Hall.

Kamil, M. (2003). *Adolescents and literacy: Reading for the 21st century.* Washington, DC: Alliance for Excellent Education.

Kasper, L., Babbitt, M., & Williams, R. (2000). *Content-based college ESL instruction.* Mahwah, NJ: Lawrence Erlbaum.

Keene, E., & Zimmerman, S. (2007). *Mosaic of thought: The power of comprehension strategy instruction.* (2nd ed.). Portsmouth, NH: Heinemman.

Kelly, P. (1991). Lexical ignorance: The main obstacle to listening comprehension with advanced foreign language learners. *International Review of Applied Linguistics in Language Teaching, 29,* 135–149.

Kinsella, K. (2007). *Rigorous and accountable academic discussion with the rbook.* Retrieved March 19, 2009, from http://teacher.scholastic.com/products/read180/pdfs/Kinsella_NSI_07_rBooks.pdf

Kirsch, I., de Jong, J., Lafontaine, D., McQueen, J., Mendelovits, J., & Monseur, C. (2002). *Reading for change: Performance and engagement across countries: Results from PISA 2000, OECD.* Retrieved March 19, 2009, from http://books.google.com/books?hl=en&lr=&id=T73yzDPuDRAC&oi=fnd&pg=PP6&dq=kirsch+oecd+2002+reading+for+change+performance+and+engagement+across+countries+results+from+pisa+2000+i-kirsch&ots=CN9sFESKp6&sig=209YI8nZ1PXfpvVHH3t4TxOX4Aw#PPA1,M1

Langer, J. (2001, Winter). Beating the odds: Teaching middle and high school students to read and write well. *American Educational Research Journal, 38*(4), 837–880.

Lapp, D., Flood, J., Brock, C., & Fisher, D. (2006). *Teaching reading to every child.* Mahwah, NJ: Lawrence Erlbaum.

Learning First Alliance. (2000). *Every child reading: A professional reading guide.* Washington, DC: Author.

Learning 24/7. (2005, April 7). *Classroom observation study.* Study presented at the meeting of the National Conference on Standards and Assessment, Las Vegas, NV.

Lyon, R. (2001). *Measuring success: Using assessments and accountability to raise student achievement.* Washington, DC: Subcommittee on Education Reform, Committee on Education and the Workforce, U.S. House of Representatives.

Marzano, R. (2004). *Building background knowledge for academic achievement: Research on what works in schools.* Alexandria, VA: Association for Supervision and Curriculum Development.

Marzano, R. (2007). *The art and science of teaching: A comprehensive framework for effective instruction.* Alexandria, VA: Association of Supervision and Curriculum Development.

McGregor, K. (2004). Developmental dependencies between lexical semantics and reading. In C. Stone, E. Silliman, B. Ehren, & K. Apel (Eds.), *Handbook of language and literacy* (pp. 302–317). New York: Guilford Press.

Meyer, B. (2003). Text coherence and readability. *Topics in Language Disorders, 23,* 204–221.

Moats, L. (2000). *Speech to print: Language essentials for teachers.* Baltimore: Brookes.

Moxley, D., & Taylor, R. (2006). *Literacy coaching: A handbook for school leaders.* Thousand Oaks, CA: Corwin.

Murphy, P., & Edwards, M. (2005, April). What the studies tell us: A meta-analysis of discussion approaches. In I. Wilkinson (Chair), *Making sense of group discussions designed to promote high-level comprehension of texts.* Symposium presented at the annual meeting of the American Educational Research Association, Montreal, Canada.

Muter, V., Hulme, C., Snowling, M., & Stevenson, J. (2004, September). Phonemes, rimes, vocabulary, and grammatical skills as foundations of early reading development: Evidence from a longitudinal study. *Developmental Psychology, 40*(5), 665–681.

Nagy, W. E., & Anderson, R. C. (1984). How many words are there in printed English? *Reading Research Quarterly, 19,* 304–330.

Nation, P. (1990). *Teaching and learning vocabulary.* New York: Newbury House.

National Association of State Boards of Education. (2005). *Reading at risk: The state response to the crisis in adolescent literacy.* Alexandria, VA: Author.

National Reading Panel. (2000). *Report of the National Reading Panel: Reports of the subgroups.* Washington, DC: U.S. Department of Health and Human Services, National Institute of Health.

National Testing Services. (2007). *California Standards Test.* Princeton, NJ: Author. Available from http://www.startest.org/cst.html

Newall, G., & Eisner, M. (2002). *School house rock* [television series]. Burbank, CA: Walt Disney Video.

Nichols, R. (1948). Factors in listening comprehension. *Speech Monographs, 15.*

Ogle, D., Klemp, R., & McBride, B. (2007). *Building literacy in social studies: Strategies for improving comprehension and critical thinking.* Alexandria, VA: Association for Supervision and Curriculum Development.

Olson, M., & Gee, T. (1991). *Teaching reading skills in secondary school,* Scranton, PA: Intext Educational.

Orfield, G., Losen, D., Wald, J., & Swanson, C. (2004). *Losing our future: How minority youth are being left behind by the graduation rate crisis.* New York: The Civil Rights Project at Harvard University, The Urban Institute Advocates for Children of New York, and The Civil Society Institute.

Pauk, W. (1997). *How to study in college.* Boston: Houghton Mifflin.

Pearson, P., Hiebert, E., & Kamil, M. (2007). Vocabulary assessment: What we know and what we need to know. *Reading Research Quarterly, 42*, 282–296.

Perkins-Gough, D. (2002, November). RAND report on reading comprehension [special report]. *Educational Leadership 60*, 92.

Phillips, S. (2005). Assessment literacy. *Policy watch: Society for the Advancement of Excellence in Education.*

Pinkus, L. (2008). *Using early warning data to improve graduation rates: Closing cracks in the education system.* New York: Carnegie Corporation.

Pollock, J. (2007). *Improving student learning one teacher at a time.* Alexandria, VA: Association of Supervision and Curriculum Development.

Powers, D. (1985). *A survey of academic demands related to listening skills* (TOEFL Research Report No. 20). Princeton, NJ: Educational Testing Service.

Raphael, T. E. (1986). Teaching question-answer relationships. *The Reading Teacher, 39*, 516–520.

Readance, J. E., Bean, T. W., & Baldwin, R. S. (2004). *Content-area literacy: An integrated approach.* Dubuque, IA: Kendall Hunt.

Richards, J. (1983). Listening comprehension: Approach, design, procedure. *TESOL Quarterly, 17*(2), 219–240.

Rickford, J. (1999). *African American vernacular English.* San Francisco: Wiley-Blackwell.

Rinehart, H., & Winston, S. (2006). *Modern Biology.* Orlando, FL: Harcourt School.

Rog, L. (2003). *Guided reading basics: Organizing, managing, and implementing a balanced literacy program in K–3.* Portland, ME: Stenhouse.

Roit, M. (2006). Essential comprehension strategies for English learners. In T. Young & N. Hadaway (Eds.), *Supporting the literacy development of English Learners: Increasing success in all classrooms* (pp. 80–95). Newark, DE: International Reading Association.

Rose, R. (2004). *The relative contribution of syntactic and semantic prominence in pronoun reference resolution.* Paper presented at Midwest Computational Linguistics Conference, Bloomington, IN.

Rosenblatt, L. (1991). Literary theory. In J. Flood, J. Jensen, D. Lapp, & J. Squire (Eds.), *Handbook of research on teaching the English language arts* (pp. 57–62). New York: Macmillan.

Rosenshine, B. (1997). Chapter 10. In J. W. Lloyd, E. J. Kame'enui, & D. Chard (Eds.), *Issues in educating students with disabilities* (pp. 197–221). Mahwah, NJ: Lawrence Erlbaum.

Rosenshine, B., & Meister, C. (1994). Reciprocal teaching: A review of the research. *Review of Educational Research, 64*, 479–531.

Rost, M. (1990). *Listening in language learning.* London: Longman.

Rounds, P. (1987). Characterizing successful classroom discourse for NNS teaching assistant training. *TESOL Quarterly, 21*(4), 643–671.

Routman, R. (1994). *Invitations: Changing as teachers and learners K–12.* Portsmouth, NH: Heinemann.

Rubin, J. (1994). A review of second language listening comprehension research. *The Modern Language Journal 78*(2), 199–221.

Sarosy, P., & Sherak, K. (2006). *Lecture ready: Strategies for academic listening, note-taking, and discussion: Book 2.* Oxford, UK: Oxford University Press.

Saunders, W., & Goldenberg, C. (2007). The effects of an instructional conversation on transition students' concepts of friendship and story comprehension. In R. Horowitz (Ed.), *The evolution of talk about text: Knowing the world through classroom discourse* (pp. 221–252). Newark, DE: International Reading Association.

Scarcella, R. (2003). *Academic English: A conceptual framework.* Irvine, CA: UC-LMRI.

Schleppegrell, M. (2004). *The language of schooling: A functional linguistic perspective.* Mahwah, NJ: Lawrence Erlbaum.

Schleppegrell, M. (2007, April). The Linguistic challenges of mathematics teaching and learning: A research review. *Reading and Writing Quarterly, 23*(2), 139–159.

Schleppegrell, M., & Colombi, C. (2002). *Developing advanced language in first and second languages: Meaning with power.* Mahwah, NJ: Lawrence Erlbaum.

Schmoker, M. (2001). *The results fieldbook: Practical strategies from dramatically improved schools.* Alexandria, VA: Association of Supervision and Curriculum Development.

Schmoker, M. (2006). *Results now: How we can achieve unprecedented improvements in teaching and learning.* Alexandria, VA: Association of Supervision and Curriculum Development.

Searle, J. (2005). Children of the code interview. *Children of the Code.* Retrieved March 20, 2009, from http://www.children ofthecode.org/interviews/pdfs/Searle.pdf

Sheorey, R., & Mokhtari, K. (2001). Coping with academic materials: Differences in the reading strategies of native and non-native readers. *System, 29*, 431–449.

Simpson, P. (2003, March). Language, register and power. *Literacy Today, 34*(1), 4–5.

Sirota. A. (2007, May 30). *UCLA programs reach out to community Center for Community Partnerships works toward establishing good educational connection with L.A.* Retrieved March 20, 2009, from http://dailybruin.com/news/2007/may/30/ucla_ programs_reach_out_community/

Snow, C. (2002). *Reading for understanding: Toward an R & D program in reading comprehension.* New York: RAND.

Snow, C., & Biancarosa, G. (2003). *Reading next: A vision for action and research in middle and high school.* Washington, DC: Alliance for Excellent Education.

Snow, C., Griffin, P., & Burns, M. (2005). *Knowledge to support the teaching of reading: Preparing teachers for a changing world.* San Francisco: Jossey-Bass.

Snow, C., & Kim, S. (2007). Large problem spaces: The challenge of vocabulary for English language learners. In R. Wagner, A. Muse, & K. Tannenbaum (Eds.), *Vocabulary acquisition: Implications for reading comprehension* (pp. 123–139). New York: Guilford Press.

Stahl, S. (1999). *Vocabulary development.* Cambridge, MA: Brookline Books.

Stahl, S., & Nagy, W. (2005). *Teaching word meanings.* Mahwah, NJ: Lawrence Erlbaum.

Stanovich, K. (1993). Does reading make you smarter? Literacy and the development of verbal intelligence. In H. Reese (Ed.), *Advances in child development and behavior Vol. 24* (pp. 133–180). San Diego, CA: Academic Press.

Stevens, R. A., Butler, F. A., & Castellon-Wellington, M. (2000). *Academic language and content assessment: Measuring the progress of ELLs* (CSE Tech. Report No. 552). Los Angeles: University of California. CRESST.

Stronge, J. (2007). *Qualities of effective teachers* (2nd ed.). Alexandria, VA: Association of Supervision and Curriculum Development.

Swartz, R., Costa, A., Beyer, B., Regan, R., & Kallick, B. (2007). *Thinking-based learning: Activating students' potential.* Norwood, MA: Christopher-Gordon.

Taba, H. (1967). *Teacher's handbook for elementary social studies.* Reading, MA: Addison-Wesley.

Taylor, B., & Pearson, P. (2002). *Teaching reading: Effective schools, accomplished teachers.* Mahwah, NJ: Lawrence Erlbaum.

Torgeson, J., Houston, D., Rissman, L., Decker, S., Roberts, G., Vaughn, S., et al. (2007). *Academic literacy instruction for adolescents: A guidance document from the Center on Instruction.* Portsmouth, NH: RMC Research Corporation, Center on Instruction.

Tough, P. (2008). *Whatever it takes: Geoffrey Canada's quest to change Harlem and America.* Boston: Houghton Mifflin.

Trosborg, A. (1997). Text typology: Register, genre and text type. In A. Trosborg, (Ed.), *Text Typology and Translation* (pp. 3–24). Philadelphia: J. Benjamins.

Wagner, T. (2008). *The global achievement gap.* New York: Basic Books.

Wilhelm, J. (2001). *Improving comprehension with think-aloud strategies: Modeling what good readers do.* New York: Scholastic.

Wilkinson, I., & Reninger, K. (2005, February). *Who's doing the talking and why does it matter? Small group discussions about literature to promote high-level thinking about texts* (Tech. Rep. No. 2). Dublin Annual Literacy Conference, Columbus, Ohio.

Willingham, D., (2006). How knowledge helps: It speeds and strengthens reading comprehension, learning—and thinking. *American Educator.* Retrieved March 20, 2009, from http://www.aft.org/pubs-reports/american_educator/issues/spring06/willingham.htm

Wolfram, W., Adger, C., & Christian, D. (1999). *Dialects in schools and communities.* Mahwah, NJ: Lawrence Erlbaum Associates.

Wong-Fillmore, L. (2007). *Resource: Academic language.* Sonoma, CA: SCOE.

Index

CORWIN
A SAGE Company

The Corwin logo—a raven striding across an open book—represents the union of courage and learning. Corwin is committed to improving education for all learners by publishing books and other professional development resources for those serving the field of PreK–12 education. By providing practical, hands-on materials, Corwin continues to carry out the promise of its motto: **"Helping Educators Do Their Work Better."**